Tanzanian Cookbook
Authentic Recipes
THE RICH AND DIVERSE FLAVORS OF TANZANIA

FATMA S. NGOWI

TANZANIAN COOKBOOK
Uncover the Rich and Diverse Flavors of Tanzania.

© Fatma S. Ngowi
© E.G.P. Editorial
   ISBN-13: 9798329767179

Copyright © 2024
All rights reserved.

FLAVOURS THAT CROSS BORDERS

From my earliest memories, the tales of Tanzania and the soothing rhythms of traditional Ngoma music were ever-present, forging a profound bond with my heritage despite being far from my grandmother's native land. My grandmother, a beacon of resilience and optimism, along with my grandfather, decided in the 1950s that New York would become their new sanctuary, a place to pursue greater opportunities for their descendants, becoming part of the vibrant and diverse Tanzanian community in Queens.

The decision to traverse seas and settle in a foreign territory was formidable; yet, my grandmother's spirit and hopeful outlook never wavered. Her stories taught me the importance of maintaining our cultural and ancestral roots, particularly through cuisine. My grandmother's kitchen turned into a sanctuary of scents and tastes, crafted not merely as nourishment but as bridges to the soul, connecting us with our Tanzanian heritage.

My grandmother believed that cooking was more than just food preparation; it was an act of love, a way to preserve our culture and pass down our narratives to future generations. Each recipe she shared was steeped in a story, a lesson, or a reminiscence of Tanzania, making every meal a festivity of our identity.

The influence of Tanzanian cuisine in my life was profoundly shaped not only by my grandmother's teachings but also by books from that era that celebrated the richness and diversity of our culinary traditions. Their inspirational nature was crucial for my grandmother to perfect and innovate her dishes, which became the centerpiece of our family gatherings in New York.

Now, as an adult and author of this book, my goal is to safeguard and promote my grandmother's culinary legacy. Although she has passed, her spirit and wisdom continue to guide me each time I prepare one of her dishes. This book is crafted as an homage to her, to her life of courage, love, and passion for cooking, aiming to inspire others to discover the joy and unity found in the culinary arts.

Through this book, I hope readers not only learn to master the art of preparing authentic Tanzanian dishes but also to appreciate the dedication and care my grandmother put into each recipe. May this work serve as a bridge between generations and cultures, demonstrating that, no matter where we are, cooking can create a haven for both the heart and the mind.

TABLE OF CONTENTS

BREAKFASTS 9
APPETIZERS... 17
SOUPS 27
STEWS 43
BEEF DISHES 60
PORK DISHES 77
CHICKEN DISHES 94
GOAT DISHES 111
SEAFOOD DISHES 128
RICE DISHES 145
BEANS 157
LEGUMES 173
SALADS... 191
DESSERTS 200
RECIPE LIST 214

BREAKFASTS

Tanzanian breakfasts stand out for their rich blend of flavors and nutritional benefits, setting them apart from typical morning meals. Ingredients like ripe plantains, uji (a nutritious porridge made from millet or sorghum), and chapati fill the morning air with enticing aromas. These staples not only provide a burst of energy but are also packed with vitamins and minerals essential for a healthy start to the day.

The versatility of Tanzanian breakfast dishes allows for a wide range of culinary creativity and adaptability to dietary needs. From the light and savory vitumbua (rice pancakes) to the hearty and filling ndizi na nyama (plantains with meat), there's a breakfast option to satisfy every palate. Each dish showcases the rich culinary traditions of Tanzania, making breakfast not just a meal but a cultural experience.

Tanzanian breakfasts are designed to energize and nourish. They perfectly balance taste and health, making them an ideal choice for those seeking a wholesome diet.

CHAPATI

Ingredients

- Flour - 2 cups.
- Water - 3/4 cup.
- Salt - 1/2 tsp.
- Oil - 2 tbsp.

Instructions

1. Mix flour and salt in a bowl.

2. Gradually add water and knead into a soft dough.

3. Let the dough rest for 30 minutes.

4. Divide the dough into small balls.

5. Roll out each ball into a thin circle.

6. Heat a pan and cook each chapati until golden brown, brushing with oil.

MANDAZI

Ingredients

- Flour - 3 cups.
- Sugar - 1/2 cup.
- Baking powder - 2 tsp.
- Cardamom powder - 1 tsp.
- Egg - 1.
- Coconut milk - 1 cup.
- Oil - for frying.

Instructions

1. Mix flour, sugar, baking powder, and cardamom in a bowl.

2. Beat the egg and add to the mixture.

3. Gradually add coconut milk and knead into a dough.

4. Roll out the dough and cut into desired shapes.

5. Heat oil in a pan and fry the mandazi until golden brown.

6. Drain on paper towels and serve warm.

VITUMBUA (RICE PANCAKES)

Ingredients

- Rice - 2 cups.
- Coconut milk - 1 cup.
- Sugar - 1/2 cup.
- Yeast - 1 tsp.
- Cardamom powder - 1 tsp.
- Oil - for frying.

Instructions

1. Soak rice in water for at least 4 hours.

2. Drain the rice and blend with coconut milk until smooth.

3. Add sugar, yeast, and cardamom powder to the mixture.

4. Let the batter rest for 1 hour to rise.

5. Heat a little oil in a pan and pour small amounts of batter to form pancakes.

6. Cook until golden brown on both sides.

UJI (PORRIDGE)

Ingredients

- Millet flour - 1 cup.
- Water - 4 cups.
- Sugar - to taste.

- Milk - optional, for serving.

Instructions

1. Mix millet flour with a little water to make a smooth paste.

2. Boil the remaining water in a pot.

3. Gradually add the millet paste to the boiling water, stirring continuously.

4. Cook for 15-20 minutes until thickened.

5. Add sugar to taste and serve with milk if desired.

MAANDAZI

Ingredients

- Flour - 4 cups.
- Sugar - 1/2 cup.
- Butter - 4 tbsp.
- Yeast - 2 tsp.
- Coconut milk - 1 cup.
- Warm water - 1/2 cup.
- Oil - for frying.

Instructions

1. Mix yeast with warm water and let it foam.

2. In a bowl, mix flour, sugar, and butter.

3. Add the yeast mixture and coconut milk to the flour mixture and knead into a dough.

4. Let the dough rise for 1 hour.

5. Roll out the dough and cut into desired shapes.

6. Heat oil in a pan and fry the maandazi until golden brown.

7. Drain on paper towels and serve warm.

NDIZI KAANGA (FRIED BANANAS)

Ingredients

- Bananas - 4, ripe but firm.
- Oil - for frying.
- Sugar - 2 tbsp.
- Cinnamon powder - 1 tsp.

Instructions

1. Peel and slice the bananas lengthwise.

2. Heat oil in a pan over medium heat.

3. Fry the banana slices until golden brown on both sides.

4. Remove from oil and drain on paper towels.

5. Sprinkle with sugar and cinnamon while still warm.

6. Serve immediately.

MAHAMRI (COCONUT DOUGHNUTS)

Ingredients

- Flour - 4 cups.

- Sugar - 1/2 cup.
- Yeast - 2 tsp.
- Cardamom powder - 1 tsp.
- Coconut milk - 1 cup.
- Warm water - 1/2 cup.
- Oil - for frying.

Instructions

1. Mix yeast with warm water and let it foam.

2. In a bowl, mix flour, sugar, and cardamom powder.

3. Add the yeast mixture and coconut milk to the flour mixture and knead into a dough.

4. Let the dough rise for 1 hour.

5. Roll out the dough and cut into desired shapes.

6. Heat oil in a pan and fry the mahamri until golden brown.

7. Drain on paper towels and serve warm.

MBAAZI
(PIGEON PEAS IN COCONUT SAUCE)

Ingredients

- Pigeon peas - 2 cups, cooked.
- Coconut milk - 1 cup.
- Onion - 1, chopped.
- Tomato - 1, chopped.
- Garlic - 2 cloves, minced.
- Oil - 2 tbsp.
- Salt - to taste.

- Pepper - to taste.

Instructions

1. Heat oil in a pan over medium heat.

2. Sauté onions until translucent.

3. Add garlic and tomatoes, and cook until soft.

4. Add cooked pigeon peas and coconut milk.

5. Season with salt and pepper.

6. Simmer for 10-15 minutes until the sauce thickens.

7. Serve hot with rice or chapati.

KASHATA
(COCONUT AND PEANUT BARS)

Ingredients

- Grated coconut - 1 cup.
- Peanuts - 1 cup, roasted and chopped.
- Sugar - 1 cup.
- Water - 1/2 cup.

Instructions

1. In a pan, combine sugar and water over medium heat.

2. Cook until the sugar dissolves and forms a syrup.

3. Add grated coconut and peanuts to the syrup.

4. Stir continuously until the mixture thickens.

5. Pour the mixture onto a greased tray and flatten it.

6. Let it cool and harden, then cut into bars.

7. Store in an airtight container.

BAGIA ZA DENGU (LENTIL FRITTERS)

Ingredients

- Green lentils - 2 cups, soaked and cooked.
- Onion - 1, chopped.
- Garlic - 3 cloves, minced.
- Cumin powder - 1 tsp.
- Coriander powder - 1 tsp.
- Chili powder - 1/2 tsp.
- Salt - to taste.
- Oil - for frying.

Instructions

1. Mash the cooked lentils in a bowl.

2. Add chopped onions, garlic, and spices to the lentils.

3. Mix well and form into small balls or patties.

4. Heat oil in a pan over medium heat.

5. Fry the lentil fritters until golden brown on all sides.

6. Drain on paper towels and serve hot.

APPETIZERS

Tanzanian appetizers are celebrated for their vibrant flavors and nutritional richness, distinguishing them from appetizers found in other cuisines. These starters often incorporate fresh vegetables, grains, and lean proteins, such as samaki (fish), which are not only delicious but also packed with essential nutrients. The use of spices like turmeric and cloves adds depth to the dishes while boosting their health benefits.

The variety in Tanzanian appetizers allows them to adapt to various dietary preferences and culinary traditions. From mchemsho, a delicately boiled mix of vegetables and meat, to kachumbari, a refreshing tomato and onion salad, each appetizer offers a unique taste of Tanzanian culture. These dishes demonstrate how Tanzanian cuisine utilizes local ingredients to create simple yet satisfying starters.

Appetizers in Tanzanian cuisine are designed to whet the appetite while contributing to a balanced diet. Their preparation emphasizes the natural flavors and nutritional values of the ingredients, making them a perfect introduction to a healthy meal.

MISHKAKI (SKEWERS)

Ingredients

- Beef or chicken - 1 lb, cubed.
- Garlic - 3 cloves, minced.
- Ginger - 1 tbsp, minced.
- Lemon juice - 2 tbsp.
- Yogurt - 1/2 cup.
- Turmeric powder - 1 tsp.

- Paprika - 1 tsp.
- Salt - to taste.
- Oil - for grilling.
- Skewers - as needed.

Instructions

1. In a bowl, mix garlic, ginger, lemon juice, yogurt, turmeric powder, paprika, and salt.

2. Add the meat cubes to the marinade and mix well.

3. Marinate for at least 2 hours or overnight in the refrigerator.

4. Thread the marinated meat onto skewers.

5. Preheat the grill and brush with oil.

6. Grill the skewers over medium heat, turning occasionally, until the meat is cooked through and charred.

7. Serve hot with a side of chutney or salad.

SAMAKI WA KUPAKA (COCONUT FISH)

Ingredients

- Fish fillets - 4.
- Coconut milk - 1 cup.
- Garlic - 2 cloves, minced.
- Ginger - 1 tbsp, minced.
- Lemon juice - 2 tbsp.
- Cumin powder - 1 tsp.
- Turmeric powder - 1 tsp.
- Salt - to taste.

- Oil - 2 tbsp.

Instructions

1. In a bowl, mix coconut milk, garlic, ginger, lemon juice, cumin powder, turmeric powder, and salt.

2. Marinate the fish fillets in the coconut mixture for at least 1 hour.

3. Heat oil in a pan over medium heat.

4. Cook the marinated fish fillets until golden brown on both sides and cooked through.

5. Serve hot with coconut sauce drizzled on top.

BAJIA (CHICKPEA FRITTERS)

Ingredients

- Chickpea flour - 1 cup.
- Onion - 1, finely chopped.
- Garlic - 2 cloves, minced.
- Cumin seeds - 1 tsp.
- Coriander leaves - 1/4 cup, chopped.
- Green chilies - 2, finely chopped.
- Salt - to taste.
- Water - as needed.
- Oil - for frying.

Instructions

1. In a bowl, mix chickpea flour, onion, garlic, cumin seeds, coriander leaves, green chilies, and salt.

2. Gradually add water to form a thick batter.

3. Heat oil in a pan over medium heat.

4. Drop spoonfuls of batter into the hot oil and fry until golden brown and crispy.

5. Drain on paper towels and serve hot with chutney or sauce.

KACHORI (SPICED POTATO BALLS)

Ingredients

- Potatoes - 4, boiled and mashed.
- Peas - 1/2 cup, boiled.
- Onion - 1, finely chopped.
- Garlic - 2 cloves, minced.
- Cumin powder - 1 tsp.
- Coriander powder - 1 tsp.
- Garam masala - 1/2 tsp.
- Salt - to taste.
- Flour - for coating.
- Oil - for frying.

Instructions

1. In a bowl, mix mashed potatoes, peas, onion, garlic, cumin powder, coriander powder, garam masala, and salt.

2. Form the mixture into small balls.

3. Roll the balls in flour to coat evenly.

4. Heat oil in a pan over medium heat.

5. Fry the potato balls until golden brown and crispy.

6. Drain on paper towels and serve hot with chutney or sauce.

MEAT SAMBUSA

Ingredients

- Ground meat (beef or lamb) - 1 lb.
- Onion - 1, finely chopped.
- Garlic - 2 cloves, minced.
- Ginger - 1 tbsp, minced.
- Green chilies - 2, finely chopped.
- Cumin powder - 1 tsp.
- Coriander powder - 1 tsp.
- Salt - to taste.
- Phyllo pastry sheets - as needed.
- Oil - for frying.

Instructions

1. Heat oil in a pan over medium heat.

2. Sauté onion, garlic, and ginger until fragrant.

3. Add ground meat and cook until browned.

4. Add green chilies, cumin powder, coriander powder, and salt.

5. Cook until the meat is fully cooked and the mixture is dry.

6. Let the mixture cool.

7. Cut phyllo pastry sheets into strips.

8. Place a spoonful of the meat mixture at one end of each

strip and fold into a triangular shape.

9. Seal the edges with a little water.

10. Heat oil in a pan and fry the sambusas until golden brown and crispy.

11. Drain on paper towels and serve hot with chutney or sauce.

MCHICHA
(SPINACH AND PEANUT CURRY)

Ingredients

- Spinach - 1 bunch, chopped.
- Peanut butter - 1/2 cup.
- Onion - 1, finely chopped.
- Tomato - 1, chopped.
- Garlic - 2 cloves, minced.
- Ginger - 1 tsp, minced.
- Salt - to taste.
- Oil - 2 tbsp.
- Water - 1 cup.

Instructions

1. Heat oil in a pan over medium heat.

2. Sauté onions until translucent.

3. Add garlic and ginger, and cook for 1-2 minutes.

4. Add chopped tomatoes and cook until soft.

5. Stir in peanut butter and water, and mix well.

6. Add chopped spinach and cook until wilted.

7. Season with salt and simmer for 10 minutes.

8. Serve hot with rice or chapati.

NDIZI NYAMA
(PLANTAINS WITH MEAT)

Ingredients

- Plantains - 4, ripe but firm, peeled and sliced.
- Beef or lamb - 1 lb, cubed.
- Onion - 1, finely chopped.
- Garlic - 2 cloves, minced.
- Ginger - 1 tbsp, minced.
- Tomato - 1, chopped.
- Turmeric powder - 1 tsp.
- Cumin powder - 1 tsp.
- Salt - to taste.
- Oil - 2 tbsp.
- Water - 2 cups.

Instructions

1. Heat oil in a pot over medium heat.

2. Sauté onions until golden brown.

3. Add garlic and ginger, and cook for 1-2 minutes.

4. Add beef or lamb and brown on all sides.

5. Stir in chopped tomatoes, turmeric, cumin, and salt.

6. Add water and bring to a boil.

7. Reduce heat and simmer until the meat is tender.

8. Add sliced plantains and cook until soft.

9. Serve hot with rice or ugali.

ACHARI (PICKLED MANGO)

Ingredients

- Mangoes - 3, raw, peeled and sliced.
- Mustard seeds - 1 tbsp.
- Fenugreek seeds - 1 tsp.
- Turmeric powder - 1 tsp.
- Chili powder - 1 tbsp.
- Salt - to taste.
- Oil - 1/4 cup.
- Vinegar - 1/2 cup.

Instructions

1. In a pan, heat oil over medium heat.

2. Add mustard seeds and fenugreek seeds, and cook until they begin to pop.

3. Add turmeric powder, chili powder, and salt, and mix well.

4. Add sliced mangoes and stir to coat with spices.

5. Cook for 5-7 minutes until the mangoes soften.

6. Remove from heat and add vinegar.

7. Mix well and let cool.

8. Store in a sterilized jar and refrigerate for up to a month.

BHAJIA ZA DENGU
(LENTIL FRITTERS)

Ingredients

- Green lentils - 2 cups, soaked and cooked.
- Onion - 1, chopped.
- Garlic - 3 cloves, minced.
- Cumin powder - 1 tsp.
- Coriander powder - 1 tsp.
- Chili powder - 1/2 tsp.
- Salt - to taste.
- Oil - for frying.

Instructions

1. Mash the cooked lentils in a bowl.

2. Add chopped onions, garlic, and spices to the lentils.

3. Mix well and form into small balls or patties.

4. Heat oil in a pan over medium heat.

5. Fry the lentil fritters until golden brown on all sides.

6. Drain on paper towels and serve hot.

PWEZA WA NAZI
(OCTOPUS IN COCONUT)

Ingredients

- Octopus - 1 lb, cleaned and cut into pieces.
- Coconut milk - 1 cup.
- Onion - 1, finely chopped.
- Garlic - 2 cloves, minced.
- Ginger - 1 tbsp, minced.
- Tomato - 1, chopped.
- Turmeric powder - 1 tsp.
- Cumin powder - 1 tsp.
- Salt - to taste.
- Oil - 2 tbsp.

Instructions

1. Heat oil in a pot over medium heat.

2. Sauté onions until golden brown.

3. Add garlic and ginger, and cook for 1-2 minutes.

4. Add octopus pieces and cook until they turn opaque.

5. Stir in chopped tomatoes, turmeric, cumin, and salt.

6. Add coconut milk and bring to a boil.

7. Reduce heat and simmer until the octopus is tender and the sauce thickens.

8. Serve hot with rice or chapati.

SOUPS

Tanzanian soups are a cornerstone of the cuisine, known for their robust flavors and nutritional content that distinctly sets them apart from other culinary traditions. Ingredients like coconut milk, beans, and various leafy greens provide a rich base for these soups, infusing them with vitamins and minerals essential for health. Additionally, the use of spices such as cardamom and cinnamon not only enhances flavor but also offers additional health benefits.

The adaptability of Tanzanian soups to incorporate seasonal and locally available ingredients demonstrates their versatility. Dishes such as mchuzi wa samaki (fish soup) and supu ya ndizi (banana soup) showcase how different regions influence the country's culinary practices while maintaining a focus on wholesome eating. Each soup is a celebration of local produce and traditional cooking methods, reflecting the diverse flavors of Tanzania.

Soups in Tanzanian cuisine are not only comforting but also align with principles of healthy eating. They are crafted to nourish the body and soul, providing a fulfilling and healthful start to any meal.

MTORI (BANANA AND BEEF SOUP)

Ingredients

- Beef - 1 lb, cubed.
- Green bananas - 4, peeled and chopped.
- Onion - 1, finely chopped.
- Garlic - 3 cloves, minced.
- Ginger - 1 tbsp, minced.

- Tomato - 1, chopped.
- Carrot - 1, chopped.
- Salt - to taste.
- Pepper - to taste.
- Water - 4 cups.
- Oil - 2 tbsp.

Instructions

1. Heat oil in a pot over medium heat.

2. Sauté onions until golden brown.

3. Add garlic and ginger, and cook for 1-2 minutes.

4. Add beef cubes and brown on all sides.

5. Stir in chopped tomatoes and cook until soft.

6. Add chopped carrots and green bananas.

7. Pour in water and bring to a boil.

8. Reduce heat and simmer until the beef is tender and bananas are soft.

9. Season with salt and pepper.

10. Serve hot.

SUPU YA NDIZI (PLANTAIN SOUP)

Ingredients

- Plantains - 3, peeled and sliced.
- Onion - 1, finely chopped.
- Garlic - 2 cloves, minced.

- Ginger - 1 tsp, minced.
- Tomato - 1, chopped.
- Carrot - 1, chopped.
- Salt - to taste.
- Pepper - to taste.
- Water - 4 cups.
- Oil - 2 tbsp.

Instructions

1. Heat oil in a pot over medium heat.

2. Sauté onions until golden brown.

3. Add garlic and ginger, and cook for 1-2 minutes.

4. Stir in chopped tomatoes and cook until soft.

5. Add chopped carrots and plantains.

6. Pour in water and bring to a boil.

7. Reduce heat and simmer until the plantains are soft.

8. Season with salt and pepper. Serve hot.

SUPU YA KUKU (CHICKEN SOUP)

Ingredients

- Chicken - 1 lb, cut into pieces.
- Onion - 1, finely chopped.
- Garlic - 3 cloves, minced.
- Ginger - 1 tbsp, minced.
- Tomato - 1, chopped.
- Carrot - 1, chopped.
- Celery - 2 stalks, chopped.

- Salt - to taste.
- Pepper - to taste.
- Water - 6 cups.
- Oil - 2 tbsp.

Instructions

1. Heat oil in a pot over medium heat.

2. Sauté onions until golden brown.

3. Add garlic and ginger, and cook for 1-2 minutes.

4. Add chicken pieces and brown on all sides.

5. Stir in chopped tomatoes and cook until soft.

6. Add chopped carrots and celery.

7. Pour in water and bring to a boil.

8. Reduce heat and simmer until the chicken is cooked through.

9. Season with salt and pepper. Serve hot.

DENGU SOUP (LENTIL SOUP)

Ingredients

- Green lentils - 1 cup, soaked and drained.
- Onion - 1, finely chopped.
- Garlic - 3 cloves, minced.
- Ginger - 1 tbsp, minced.
- Tomato - 1, chopped.
- Carrot - 1, chopped.
- Celery - 2 stalks, chopped.

- Cumin powder - 1 tsp.
- Coriander powder - 1 tsp.
- Salt - to taste.
- Pepper - to taste.
- Water - 6 cups.
- Oil - 2 tbsp.

Instructions

1. Heat oil in a pot over medium heat.

2. Sauté onions until golden brown.

3. Add garlic and ginger, and cook for 1-2 minutes.

4. Stir in chopped tomatoes and cook until soft.

5. Add chopped carrots and celery.

6. Add soaked lentils, cumin powder, and coriander powder.

7. Pour in water and bring to a boil.

8. Reduce heat and simmer until the lentils are tender.

9. Season with salt and pepper. Serve hot.

NYAMA YA KUSAGA SOUP (GROUND MEAT SOUP)

Ingredients

- Ground beef or lamb - 1 lb.
- Onion - 1, finely chopped.
- Garlic - 3 cloves, minced.
- Ginger - 1 tbsp, minced.

- Tomato - 1, chopped.
- Carrot - 1, chopped.
- Celery - 2 stalks, chopped.
- Salt - to taste.
- Pepper - to taste.
- Water - 6 cups.
- Oil - 2 tbsp.

Instructions

1. Heat oil in a pot over medium heat.

2. Sauté onions until golden brown.

3. Add garlic and ginger, and cook for 1-2 minutes.

4. Add ground meat and cook until browned.

5. Stir in chopped tomatoes and cook until soft.

6. Add chopped carrots and celery.

7. Pour in water and bring to a boil.

8. Reduce heat and simmer until the vegetables are tender.

9. Season with salt and pepper. Serve hot.

UROJO (ZANZIBAR SOUP)

Ingredients

- Potatoes - 2, peeled and cubed.
- Chickpea flour - 1/2 cup.
- Garlic - 2 cloves, minced.
- Ginger - 1 tsp, minced.

- Lemon juice - 2 tbsp.
- Turmeric powder - 1 tsp.
- Chili powder - 1 tsp.
- Salt - to taste.
- Water - 4 cups.
- Oil - 2 tbsp.

Instructions

1. Heat oil in a pot over medium heat.

2. Add garlic and ginger, and sauté for 1-2 minutes.

3. Add turmeric powder, chili powder, and salt, and mix well.

4. Stir in chickpea flour and cook for 2-3 minutes.

5. Add cubed potatoes and water, and bring to a boil.

6. Reduce heat and simmer until the potatoes are tender.

7. Add lemon juice and adjust seasoning.

8. Serve hot.

MAKANGE YA NYAMA (SPICED BEEF SOUP)

Ingredients

- Beef - 1 lb, cubed.
- Onion - 1, finely chopped.
- Garlic - 3 cloves, minced.
- Ginger - 1 tbsp, minced.
- Tomato - 1, chopped.
- Carrot - 1, chopped.

- Celery - 2 stalks, chopped.
- Cumin powder - 1 tsp.
- Coriander powder - 1 tsp.
- Salt - to taste.
- Pepper - to taste.
- Water - 6 cups.
- Oil - 2 tbsp.

Instructions

1. Heat oil in a pot over medium heat.

2. Sauté onions until golden brown.

3. Add garlic and ginger, and cook for 1-2 minutes.

4. Add beef cubes and brown on all sides.

5. Stir in chopped tomatoes, cumin powder, and coriander powder.

6. Add chopped carrots and celery.

7. Pour in water and bring to a boil.

8. Reduce heat and simmer until the beef is tender.

9. Season with salt and pepper.

10. Serve hot.

SAMAKI SOUP (FISH SOUP)

Ingredients

- Fish fillets - 1 lb, cubed.
- Onion - 1, finely chopped.

- Garlic - 2 cloves, minced.
- Ginger - 1 tsp, minced.
- Tomato - 1, chopped.
- Carrot - 1, chopped.
- Celery - 2 stalks, chopped.
- Cumin powder - 1 tsp.
- Coriander powder - 1 tsp.
- Salt - to taste.
- Pepper - to taste.
- Water - 4 cups.
- Oil - 2 tbsp.

Instructions

1. Heat oil in a pot over medium heat.

2. Sauté onions until golden brown.

3. Add garlic and ginger, and cook for 1-2 minutes.

4. Add fish fillets and cook until opaque.

5. Stir in chopped tomatoes, cumin powder, and coriander powder.

6. Add chopped carrots and celery.

7. Pour in water and bring to a boil.

8. Reduce heat and simmer until the vegetables are tender.

9. Season with salt and pepper.

10. Serve hot.

SUPU YA VIAZI (POTATO SOUP)

Ingredients

- Potatoes - 4, peeled and cubed.
- Onion - 1, finely chopped.
- Garlic - 3 cloves, minced.
- Ginger - 1 tbsp, minced.
- Carrot - 1, chopped.
- Celery - 2 stalks, chopped.
- Salt - to taste.
- Pepper - to taste.
- Water - 6 cups.
- Oil - 2 tbsp.

Instructions

1. Heat oil in a pot over medium heat.

2. Sauté onions until golden brown.

3. Add garlic and ginger, and cook for 1-2 minutes.

4. Add cubed potatoes and cook for 5 minutes.

5. Stir in chopped carrots and celery.

6. Pour in water and bring to a boil.

7. Reduce heat and simmer until the potatoes are tender.

8. Season with salt and pepper.

9. Serve hot.

SUPU YA KARANGA (PEANUT SOUP)

Ingredients

- Peanuts - 1 cup, roasted and ground.
- Onion - 1, finely chopped.
- Garlic - 3 cloves, minced.
- Ginger - 1 tbsp, minced.
- Tomato - 1, chopped.
- Carrot - 1, chopped.
- Celery - 2 stalks, chopped.
- Salt - to taste.
- Pepper - to taste.
- Water - 6 cups.
- Oil - 2 tbsp.

Instructions

1. Heat oil in a pot over medium heat.

2. Sauté onions until golden brown.

3. Add garlic and ginger, and cook for 1-2 minutes.

4. Stir in ground peanuts and cook for 3-4 minutes.

5. Add chopped tomatoes, carrots, and celery.

6. Pour in water and bring to a boil.

7. Reduce heat and simmer until the vegetables are tender.

8. Season with salt and pepper.

9. Serve hot.

MBAAZI SOUP (PIGEON PEA SOUP)

Ingredients

- Pigeon peas - 2 cups, cooked.
- Onion - 1, finely chopped.
- Garlic - 3 cloves, minced.
- Ginger - 1 tbsp, minced.
- Tomato - 1, chopped.
- Carrot - 1, chopped.
- Coconut milk - 1 cup.
- Water - 4 cups.
- Salt - to taste.
- Pepper - to taste.
- Oil - 2 tbsp.

Instructions

1. Heat oil in a pot over medium heat.
2. Sauté onions until golden brown.
3. Add garlic and ginger, and cook for 1-2 minutes.
4. Add chopped tomatoes and cook until soft.
5. Add cooked pigeon peas and chopped carrots.
6. Pour in water and bring to a boil.
7. Reduce heat and simmer for 20 minutes.
8. Stir in coconut milk and cook for another 10 minutes.
9. Season with salt and pepper.
10. Serve hot.

NG'OMBE SOUP (BEEF BONE SOUP)

Ingredients

- Beef bones - 1 lb.
- Onion - 1, chopped.
- Garlic - 3 cloves, minced.
- Ginger - 1 tbsp, minced.
- Tomato - 1, chopped.
- Carrot - 1, chopped.
- Celery - 2 stalks, chopped.
- Salt - to taste.
- Pepper - to taste.
- Water - 8 cups.
- Oil - 2 tbsp.

Instructions

1. Heat oil in a large pot over medium heat.

2. Add beef bones and brown on all sides.

3. Add onions, garlic, and ginger, and cook until onions are golden brown.

4. Add chopped tomatoes, carrots, and celery.

5. Pour in water and bring to a boil.

6. Reduce heat and simmer for 2-3 hours, skimming off any foam.

7. Season with salt and pepper.

8. Strain the soup and discard the bones and vegetables.

9. Serve hot.

KAMBA NA NAZI
(PRAWN AND COCONUT SOUP)

Ingredients

- Prawns - 1 lb, cleaned.
- Onion - 1, finely chopped.
- Garlic - 3 cloves, minced.
- Ginger - 1 tbsp, minced.
- Tomato - 1, chopped.
- Coconut milk - 1 cup.
- Water - 4 cups.
- Salt - to taste.
- Pepper - to taste.
- Oil - 2 tbsp.

Instructions

1. Heat oil in a pot over medium heat.

2. Sauté onions until golden brown.

3. Add garlic and ginger, and cook for 1-2 minutes.

4. Add chopped tomatoes and cook until soft.

5. Add prawns and cook until they turn pink.

6. Pour in coconut milk and water, and bring to a boil.

7. Reduce heat and simmer for 10-15 minutes.

8. Season with salt and pepper.

9. Serve hot.

MCHUZI WA BIRINGANI
(EGGPLANT STEW)

Ingredients

- Eggplants - 2, cubed.
- Onion - 1, finely chopped.
- Garlic - 3 cloves, minced.
- Ginger - 1 tbsp, minced.
- Tomato - 1, chopped.
- Coconut milk - 1 cup.
- Water - 4 cups.
- Salt - to taste.
- Pepper - to taste.
- Oil - 2 tbsp.

Instructions

1. Heat oil in a pot over medium heat.

2. Sauté onions until golden brown.

3. Add garlic and ginger, and cook for 1-2 minutes.

4. Add chopped tomatoes and cook until soft.

5. Add cubed eggplants and cook for 5-7 minutes.

6. Pour in coconut milk and water, and bring to a boil.

7. Reduce heat and simmer until the eggplants are tender.

8. Season with salt and pepper.

9. Serve hot.

SUPU YA MATUMBO (TRIPE SOUP)

Ingredients

- Tripe - 1 lb, cleaned and cut into pieces.
- Onion - 1, chopped.
- Garlic - 3 cloves, minced.
- Ginger - 1 tbsp, minced.
- Tomato - 1, chopped.
- Carrot - 1, chopped.
- Celery - 2 stalks, chopped.
- Salt - to taste.
- Pepper - to taste.
- Water - 8 cups.
- Oil - 2 tbsp.

Instructions

1. Heat oil in a large pot over medium heat.

2. Add tripe and brown on all sides.

3. Add onions, garlic, and ginger, and cook until onions are golden brown.

4. Add chopped tomatoes, carrots, and celery.

5. Pour in water and bring to a boil.

6. Reduce heat and simmer for 2-3 hours, skimming off any foam.

7. Season with salt and pepper.

8. Serve hot.

STEWS

Tanzanian stews are a vibrant testament to the country's rich culinary landscape, known for their hearty ingredients and nourishing qualities. These stews often feature a mix of local meats, vegetables, and legumes, simmered in aromatic spices that not only enhance the flavor but also increase the dish's nutritional value. Ingredients like cassava, spinach, and pulses are staples, providing a high fiber content that is vital for a balanced diet.

The versatility of Tanzanian stews is evident in their ability to incorporate a variety of ingredients, making each dish uniquely satisfying. From the coastal seafood delights in coconut-rich sauces to inland preparations with grains and meats, these stews adapt to the available local produce. This adaptability makes them a central part of meals, celebrating Tanzania's agricultural diversity while promoting health-conscious eating.

Stews in Tanzanian cuisine serve as a flavorful foundation for a healthy lifestyle. They combine tradition and nutrition, offering warming, wholesome meals that cater to both taste and health.

NYAMA CHOMA (GRILLED MEAT)

Ingredients

- Beef or goat meat - 2 lbs, cut into pieces.
- Lemon juice - 2 tbsp.
- Garlic - 4 cloves, minced.
- Ginger - 1 tbsp, minced.
- Salt - to taste.
- Pepper - to taste.

- Oil - 2 tbsp.

Instructions

1. In a bowl, mix lemon juice, garlic, ginger, salt, pepper, and oil.

2. Add the meat pieces to the marinade and mix well.

3. Marinate for at least 2 hours or overnight in the refrigerator.

4. Preheat the grill to medium-high heat.

5. Grill the meat until cooked through and charred, turning occasionally.

6. Serve hot with a side of kachumbari (tomato and onion salad).

MCHUZI WA SAMAKI (FISH CURRY)

Ingredients

- Fish fillets - 1 lb, cut into pieces.
- Onion - 1, finely chopped.
- Garlic - 3 cloves, minced.
- Ginger - 1 tbsp, minced.
- Tomato - 2, chopped.
- Coconut milk - 1 cup.
- Turmeric powder - 1 tsp.
- Cumin powder - 1 tsp.
- Coriander powder - 1 tsp.
- Salt - to taste.
- Pepper - to taste.
- Oil - 2 tbsp.

Instructions

1. Heat oil in a pot over medium heat.

2. Sauté onions until golden brown.

3. Add garlic and ginger, and cook for 1-2 minutes.

4. Add chopped tomatoes and cook until soft.

5. Stir in turmeric, cumin, and coriander powders.

6. Add fish pieces and cook until opaque.

7. Pour in coconut milk and bring to a boil.

8. Reduce heat and simmer until the fish is cooked through.

9. Season with salt and pepper.

10. Serve hot with rice or chapati.

MCHUZI WA NYAMA (BEEF CURRY)

Ingredients

- Beef - 1 lb, cubed.
- Onion - 1, finely chopped.
- Garlic - 3 cloves, minced.
- Ginger - 1 tbsp, minced.
- Tomato - 2, chopped.
- Potato - 2, cubed.
- Carrot - 1, chopped.
- Turmeric powder - 1 tsp.
- Cumin powder - 1 tsp.
- Coriander powder - 1 tsp.

- Salt - to taste.
- Pepper - to taste.
- Water - 4 cups.
- Oil - 2 tbsp.

Instructions

1. Heat oil in a pot over medium heat.

2. Sauté onions until golden brown.

3. Add garlic and ginger, and cook for 1-2 minutes.

4. Add beef cubes and brown on all sides.

5. Add chopped tomatoes and cook until soft.

6. Stir in turmeric, cumin, and coriander powders.

7. Add potatoes and carrots, and mix well.

8. Pour in water and bring to a boil.

9. Reduce heat and simmer until the beef and vegetables are tender.

10. Season with salt and pepper.

11. Serve hot with rice or chapati.

OCTOPUS CURRY

Ingredients

- Octopus - 1 lb, cleaned and cut into pieces.
- Onion - 1, finely chopped.
- Garlic - 3 cloves, minced.

- Ginger - 1 tbsp, minced.
- Tomato - 2, chopped.
- Coconut milk - 1 cup.
- Turmeric powder - 1 tsp.
- Cumin powder - 1 tsp.
- Coriander powder - 1 tsp.
- Salt - to taste.
- Pepper - to taste.
- Water - 2 cups.
- Oil - 2 tbsp.

Instructions

1. Heat oil in a pot over medium heat.

2. Sauté onions until golden brown.

3. Add garlic and ginger, and cook for 1-2 minutes.

4. Add octopus pieces and cook until they turn opaque.

5. Add chopped tomatoes and cook until soft.

6. Stir in turmeric, cumin, and coriander powders.

7. Pour in coconut milk and water, and bring to a boil.

8. Reduce heat and simmer until the octopus is tender.

9. Season with salt and pepper.

10. Serve hot with rice or chapati.

MCHUZI WA KUKU (CHICKEN CURRY)

Ingredients

- Chicken - 1 lb, cut into pieces.
- Onion - 1, finely chopped.
- Garlic - 3 cloves, minced.
- Ginger - 1 tbsp, minced.
- Tomato - 2, chopped.
- Potato - 2, cubed.
- Carrot - 1, chopped.
- Turmeric powder - 1 tsp.
- Cumin powder - 1 tsp.
- Coriander powder - 1 tsp.
- Salt - to taste.
- Pepper - to taste.
- Water - 4 cups.
- Oil - 2 tbsp.

Instructions

1. Heat oil in a pot over medium heat.

2. Sauté onions until golden brown.

3. Add garlic and ginger, and cook for 1-2 minutes.

4. Add chicken pieces and brown on all sides.

5. Add chopped tomatoes and cook until soft.

6. Stir in turmeric, cumin, and coriander powders.

7. Add potatoes and carrots, and mix well.

8. Pour in water and bring to a boil.

9. Reduce heat and simmer until the chicken and vegetables are tender.

10. Season with salt and pepper.

11. Serve hot with rice or chapati.

BOKO BOKO HAREES (WHEAT AND MEAT PORRIDGE)

Ingredients

- Meat (beef or lamb) - 1 lb, cubed.
- Wheat grains - 1 cup, soaked overnight.
- Onion - 1, finely chopped.
- Garlic - 3 cloves, minced.
- Ginger - 1 tbsp, minced.
- Cumin powder - 1 tsp.
- Coriander powder - 1 tsp.
- Salt - to taste.
- Pepper - to taste.
- Water - 6 cups.
- Oil - 2 tbsp.

Instructions

1. Heat oil in a large pot over medium heat.

2. Sauté onions until golden brown.

3. Add garlic and ginger, and cook for 1-2 minutes.

4. Add meat cubes and brown on all sides.

5. Stir in cumin and coriander powders.

6. Add soaked wheat grains and water.

7. Bring to a boil, then reduce heat and simmer until the meat and wheat are tender, about 2-3 hours.

8. Season with salt and pepper.

9. Serve hot.

MCHUZI WA MBUZI (GOAT CURRY)

Ingredients

- Goat meat - 1 lb, cubed.
- Onion - 1, finely chopped.
- Garlic - 3 cloves, minced.
- Ginger - 1 tbsp, minced.
- Tomato - 2, chopped.
- Potato - 2, cubed.
- Carrot - 1, chopped.
- Turmeric powder - 1 tsp.
- Cumin powder - 1 tsp.
- Coriander powder - 1 tsp.
- Salt - to taste.
- Pepper - to taste.
- Water - 4 cups.
- Oil - 2 tbsp.

Instructions

1. Heat oil in a pot over medium heat.

2. Sauté onions until golden brown.

3. Add garlic and ginger, and cook for 1-2 minutes.

4. Add goat meat cubes and brown on all sides.

5. Add chopped tomatoes and cook until soft.

6. Stir in turmeric, cumin, and coriander powders.

7. Add potatoes and carrots, and mix well.

8. Pour in water and bring to a boil.

9. Reduce heat and simmer until the goat meat and vegetables are tender.

10. Season with salt and pepper.

11. Serve hot with rice or chapati.

MCHUZI WA DENGU (LENTIL STEW)

Ingredients

- Green lentils - 1 cup, soaked and drained.
- Onion - 1, finely chopped.
- Garlic - 3 cloves, minced.
- Ginger - 1 tbsp, minced.
- Tomato - 2, chopped.
- Carrot - 1, chopped.
- Celery - 2 stalks, chopped.
- Turmeric powder - 1 tsp.
- Cumin powder - 1 tsp.
- Coriander powder - 1 tsp.
- Salt - to taste.
- Pepper - to taste.
- Water - 6 cups.
- Oil - 2 tbsp.

Instructions

1. Heat oil in a pot over medium heat.

2. Sauté onions until golden brown.

3. Add garlic and ginger, and cook for 1-2 minutes.

4. Add soaked lentils, chopped tomatoes, carrots, and celery.

5. Stir in turmeric, cumin, and coriander powders.

6. Pour in water and bring to a boil.

7. Reduce heat and simmer until the lentils are tender.

8. Season with salt and pepper.

9. Serve hot.

KUKU PAKA (CHICKEN IN COCONUT)

Ingredients

- Chicken - 1 lb, cut into pieces.
- Onion - 1, finely chopped.
- Garlic - 3 cloves, minced.
- Ginger - 1 tbsp, minced.
- Tomato - 2, chopped.
- Coconut milk - 1 cup.
- Turmeric powder - 1 tsp.
- Cumin powder - 1 tsp.
- Coriander powder - 1 tsp.
- Salt - to taste.
- Pepper - to taste.
- Water - 2 cups.
- Oil - 2 tbsp.

Instructions

1. Heat oil in a pot over medium heat.

2. Sauté onions until golden brown.

3. Add garlic and ginger, and cook for 1-2 minutes.

4. Add chicken pieces and brown on all sides.

5. Add chopped tomatoes and cook until soft.

6. Stir in turmeric, cumin, and coriander powders.

7. Pour in coconut milk and water, and bring to a boil.

8. Reduce heat and simmer until the chicken is tender and the sauce thickens.

9. Season with salt and pepper.

10. Serve hot with rice or chapati.

MCHUZI WA BIRINGANI (EGGPLANT STEW)

Ingredients

- Eggplants - 2, cubed.
- Onion - 1, finely chopped.
- Garlic - 3 cloves, minced.
- Ginger - 1 tbsp, minced.
- Tomato - 2, chopped.
- Coconut milk - 1 cup.
- Turmeric powder - 1 tsp.
- Cumin powder - 1 tsp.
- Coriander powder - 1 tsp.
- Salt - to taste.
- Pepper - to taste.
- Water - 2 cups.
- Oil - 2 tbsp.

Instructions

1. Heat oil in a pot over medium heat.

2. Sauté onions until golden brown.

3. Add garlic and ginger, and cook for 1-2 minutes.

4. Add cubed eggplants and cook for 5-7 minutes.

5. Add chopped tomatoes and cook until soft.

6. Stir in turmeric, cumin, and coriander powders.

7. Pour in coconut milk and water, and bring to a boil.

8. Reduce heat and simmer until the eggplants are tender and the sauce thickens.

9. Season with salt and pepper.

10. Serve hot with rice or chapati.

MCHUZI WA NAZI (COCONUT SAUCE)

Ingredients

- Coconut milk - 2 cups.
- Onion - 1, finely chopped.
- Garlic - 3 cloves, minced.
- Ginger - 1 tbsp, minced.
- Tomato - 2, chopped.
- Green chili - 1, chopped.
- Turmeric powder - 1 tsp.
- Cumin powder - 1 tsp.
- Salt - to taste.
- Pepper - to taste.

- Oil - 2 tbsp.

Instructions

1. Heat oil in a pot over medium heat.

2. Sauté onions until golden brown.

3. Add garlic and ginger, and cook for 1-2 minutes.

4. Add chopped tomatoes and green chili, and cook until soft.

5. Stir in turmeric and cumin powders.

6. Pour in coconut milk and bring to a boil.

7. Reduce heat and simmer until the sauce thickens.

8. Season with salt and pepper.

9. Serve hot with rice or chapati.

MCHUZI WA PWEZA (OCTOPUS CURRY)

Ingredients

- Octopus - 1 lb, cleaned and cut into pieces.
- Onion - 1, finely chopped.
- Garlic - 3 cloves, minced.
- Ginger - 1 tbsp, minced.
- Tomato - 2, chopped.
- Coconut milk - 1 cup.
- Turmeric powder - 1 tsp.
- Cumin powder - 1 tsp.
- Coriander powder - 1 tsp.

- Salt - to taste.
- Pepper - to taste.
- Water - 2 cups.
- Oil - 2 tbsp.

Instructions

1. Heat oil in a pot over medium heat.
2. Sauté onions until golden brown.
3. Add garlic and ginger, and cook for 1-2 minutes.
4. Add octopus pieces and cook until they turn opaque.
5. Add chopped tomatoes and cook until soft.
6. Stir in turmeric, cumin, and coriander powders.
7. Pour in coconut milk and water, and bring to a boil.
8. Reduce heat and simmer until the octopus is tender.
9. Season with salt and pepper.
10. Serve hot with rice or chapati.

BAMIA (OKRA STEW)

Ingredients

- Okra - 1 lb, trimmed and cut into pieces.
- Onion - 1, finely chopped.
- Garlic - 3 cloves, minced.
- Ginger - 1 tbsp, minced.
- Tomato - 2, chopped.
- Cumin powder - 1 tsp.

- Coriander powder - 1 tsp.
- Turmeric powder - 1 tsp.
- Salt - to taste.
- Pepper - to taste.
- Water - 2 cups.
- Oil - 2 tbsp.

Instructions

1. Heat oil in a pot over medium heat.

2. Sauté onions until golden brown.

3. Add garlic and ginger, and cook for 1-2 minutes.

4. Add chopped tomatoes and cook until soft.

5. Stir in cumin, coriander, and turmeric powders.

6. Add okra pieces and cook for 5-7 minutes.

7. Pour in water and bring to a boil.

8. Reduce heat and simmer until the okra is tender.

9. Season with salt and pepper. Serve hot with rice or chapati.

KAMBA MCHUZI (PRAWN CURRY)

Ingredients

- Prawns - 1 lb, cleaned.
- Onion - 1, finely chopped.
- Garlic - 3 cloves, minced.
- Ginger - 1 tbsp, minced.
- Tomato - 2, chopped.

- Coconut milk - 1 cup.
- Turmeric powder - 1 tsp.
- Cumin powder - 1 tsp.
- Coriander powder - 1 tsp.
- Salt - to taste.
- Pepper - to taste.
- Water - 2 cups.
- Oil - 2 tbsp.

Instructions

1. Heat oil in a pot over medium heat.

2. Sauté onions until golden brown.

3. Add garlic and ginger, and cook for 1-2 minutes.

4. Add prawns and cook until they turn pink.

5. Add chopped tomatoes and cook until soft.

6. Stir in turmeric, cumin, and coriander powders.

7. Pour in coconut milk and water, and bring to a boil.

8. Reduce heat and simmer until the prawns are cooked through.

9. Season with salt and pepper. Serve hot with rice or chapati.

MCHUZI WA KAMBA (SHRIMP STEW)

Ingredients

- Shrimp - 1 lb, cleaned.

- Onion - 1, finely chopped.
- Garlic - 3 cloves, minced.
- Ginger - 1 tbsp, minced.
- Tomato - 2, chopped.
- Coconut milk - 1 cup.
- Turmeric powder - 1 tsp.
- Cumin powder - 1 tsp.
- Coriander powder - 1 tsp.
- Salt - to taste.
- Pepper - to taste.
- Water - 2 cups.
- Oil - 2 tbsp.

Instructions

1. Heat oil in a pot over medium heat.

2. Sauté onions until golden brown.

3. Add garlic and ginger, and cook for 1-2 minutes.

4. Add shrimp and cook until they turn pink.

5. Add chopped tomatoes and cook until soft.

6. Stir in turmeric, cumin, and coriander powders.

7. Pour in coconut milk and water, and bring to a boil.

8. Reduce heat and simmer until the shrimp are cooked through.

9. Season with salt and pepper.

10. Serve hot with rice or chapati.

BEEF DISHES

Tanzanian beef dishes are renowned for their deep flavors and the pivotal role they play in the nation's diet, offering unique takes that set them apart from other global cuisines. These dishes often utilize fresh, locally-sourced beef, cooked with a variety of indigenous spices and ingredients like tomatoes, onions, and green bananas, enhancing both the taste and nutritional value. The cooking methods, whether slow-simmered or grilled, help in retaining the natural flavors and nutrients, making these meals both delicious and wholesome.

The versatility of beef in Tanzanian cuisine is showcased through a range of dishes from nyama choma, a beloved grilled meat delicacy, to beef stews enriched with coconut milk. These preparations are not only tailored to leverage the flavors of the beef but also to complement it with grains and vegetables, creating a balanced meal. The adaptability of beef within these recipes allows it to be a staple food suitable for various occasions and dietary preferences.

Beef dishes in Tanzania are more than just a source of protein; they are a cultural expression of the community's resourcefulness and culinary heritage. They offer a fulfilling and nutritious choice for families, emphasizing a healthy approach to traditional cooking.

NYAMA CHOMA

Ingredients

- Beef - 2 lbs, cut into pieces.
- Lemon juice - 2 tbsp.
- Garlic - 4 cloves, minced.

- Ginger - 1 tbsp, minced.
- Salt - to taste.
- Pepper - to taste.
- Oil - 2 tbsp.

Instructions

1. In a bowl, mix lemon juice, garlic, ginger, salt, pepper, and oil.

2. Add the meat pieces to the marinade and mix well.

3. Marinate for at least 2 hours or overnight in the refrigerator.

4. Preheat the grill to medium-high heat.

5. Grill the meat until cooked through and charred, turning occasionally.

6. Serve hot with a side of kachumbari (tomato and onion salad).

PILAU
(SPICED RICE WITH MEAT)

Ingredients

- Beef - 1 lb, cubed.
- Basmati rice - 2 cups.
- Onion - 1, finely chopped.
- Garlic - 3 cloves, minced.
- Ginger - 1 tbsp, minced.
- Tomato - 2, chopped.
- Carrot - 1, chopped.
- Potato - 2, cubed.
- Cumin seeds - 1 tsp.

- Cardamom pods - 4.
- Cinnamon stick - 1.
- Cloves - 4.
- Salt - to taste.
- Water - 4 cups.
- Oil - 3 tbsp.

Instructions

1. Heat oil in a large pot over medium heat.

2. Sauté onions until golden brown.

3. Add garlic, ginger, and whole spices (cumin, cardamom, cinnamon, cloves) and cook for 1-2 minutes.

4. Add beef cubes and brown on all sides.

5. Stir in chopped tomatoes, carrots, and potatoes.

6. Add rice and mix well.

7. Pour in water and bring to a boil.

8. Reduce heat, cover, and simmer until the rice is cooked and the liquid is absorbed.

9. Season with salt. Serve hot.

BIRYANI

Ingredients

- Beef - 1 lb, cubed.
- Basmati rice - 2 cups.
- Onion - 1, finely chopped.
- Garlic - 3 cloves, minced.

- Ginger - 1 tbsp, minced.
- Tomato - 2, chopped.
- Yogurt - 1 cup.
- Mint leaves - 1/4 cup, chopped.
- Cilantro - 1/4 cup, chopped.
- Cumin powder - 1 tsp.
- Coriander powder - 1 tsp.
- Turmeric powder - 1/2 tsp.
- Salt - to taste.
- Water - 4 cups.
- Oil - 3 tbsp.

Instructions

1. Heat oil in a large pot over medium heat.

2. Sauté onions until golden brown.

3. Add garlic, ginger, cumin, coriander, and turmeric powders and cook for 1-2 minutes.

4. Add beef cubes and brown on all sides.

5. Stir in chopped tomatoes and yogurt.

6. Add mint leaves and cilantro.

7. Add rice and mix well.

8. Pour in water and bring to a boil.

9. Reduce heat, cover, and simmer until the rice is cooked and the liquid is absorbed.

10. Season with salt.

11. Serve hot.

BEEF KEBABS

Ingredients

- Ground beef - 1 lb.
- Onion - 1, grated.
- Garlic - 3 cloves, minced.
- Ginger - 1 tbsp, minced.
- Mint leaves - 1/4 cup, chopped.
- Cilantro - 1/4 cup, chopped.
- Cumin powder - 1 tsp.
- Coriander powder - 1 tsp.
- Chili powder - 1/2 tsp.
- Salt - to taste.
- Pepper - to taste.
- Oil - for grilling.
- Skewers - as needed.

Instructions

1. In a bowl, mix ground beef, grated onion, garlic, ginger, mint, cilantro, and spices.

2. Season with salt and pepper.

3. Shape the mixture into kebabs and thread onto skewers.

4. Preheat the grill to medium-high heat and brush with oil.

5. Grill the kebabs until cooked through and charred, turning occasionally.

6. Serve hot with a side of chutney or salad.

BEEF SAMAKI

Ingredients

- Beef - 1 lb, cubed.
- Fish fillets - 1 lb, cubed.
- Onion - 1, finely chopped.
- Garlic - 3 cloves, minced.
- Ginger - 1 tbsp, minced.
- Tomato - 2, chopped.
- Coconut milk - 1 cup.
- Turmeric powder - 1 tsp.
- Cumin powder - 1 tsp.
- Coriander powder - 1 tsp.
- Salt - to taste.
- Pepper - to taste.
- Water - 2 cups.
- Oil - 2 tbsp.

Instructions

1. Heat oil in a pot over medium heat.

2. Sauté onions until golden brown.

3. Add garlic and ginger, and cook for 1-2 minutes.

4. Add beef cubes and brown on all sides.

5. Add chopped tomatoes and cook until soft.

6. Stir in turmeric, cumin, and coriander powders.

7. Add fish cubes and cook until they turn opaque.

8. Pour in coconut milk and water, and bring to a boil.

9. Reduce heat and simmer until the beef and fish are cooked through and the sauce thickens.

10. Season with salt and pepper.

11. Serve hot with rice or chapati.

KITIMOTO (PORK)

Ingredients

- Pork - 2 lbs, cut into pieces.
- Garlic - 4 cloves, minced.
- Ginger - 1 tbsp, minced.
- Lemon juice - 2 tbsp.
- Salt - to taste.
- Pepper - to taste.
- Oil - 2 tbsp.
- Onion - 1, sliced.
- Tomato - 2, chopped.
- Green chili - 1, chopped.

Instructions

1. In a bowl, mix garlic, ginger, lemon juice, salt, and pepper.

2. Add pork pieces to the marinade and mix well.

3. Marinate for at least 2 hours or overnight in the refrigerator.

4. Heat oil in a pot over medium heat.

5. Add marinated pork and cook until browned on all sides.

6. Add sliced onions, chopped tomatoes, and green chili.

7. Cook until the vegetables are soft and the pork is cooked through.

8. Serve hot with rice or chapati.

NYAMA YA KUKAANGA (FRIED BEEF)

Ingredients

- Beef - 1 lb, thinly sliced.
- Onion - 1, sliced.
- Garlic - 3 cloves, minced.
- Ginger - 1 tbsp, minced.
- Green bell pepper - 1, sliced.
- Tomato - 2, chopped.
- Soy sauce - 2 tbsp.
- Salt - to taste.
- Pepper - to taste.
- Oil - 3 tbsp.

Instructions

1. Heat oil in a large skillet over medium heat.

2. Add sliced onions and cook until golden brown.

3. Add garlic and ginger, and cook for 1-2 minutes.

4. Add sliced beef and stir-fry until browned.

5. Add green bell pepper and cook for another 2-3 minutes.

6. Stir in chopped tomatoes and soy sauce.

7. Cook until the beef is tender and the vegetables are soft.

8. Season with salt and pepper.

9. Serve hot with rice or chapati.

BEEF STEW

Ingredients

- Beef - 1 lb, cubed.
- Onion - 1, chopped.
- Garlic - 3 cloves, minced.
- Ginger - 1 tbsp, minced.
- Tomato - 2, chopped.
- Potato - 2, cubed.
- Carrot - 1, sliced.
- Beef broth - 4 cups.
- Salt - to taste.
- Pepper - to taste.
- Oil - 3 tbsp.

Instructions

1. Heat oil in a pot over medium heat.

2. Add chopped onions and cook until golden brown.

3. Add garlic and ginger, and cook for 1-2 minutes.

4. Add beef cubes and brown on all sides.

5. Add chopped tomatoes, potatoes, and carrots.

6. Pour in beef broth and bring to a boil.

7. Reduce heat and simmer until the beef and vegetables are tender.

8. Season with salt and pepper.

9. Serve hot with rice or chapati.

MKATE WA NYAMA (MEAT BREAD)

Ingredients

- Ground beef - 1 lb.
- Onion - 1, finely chopped.
- Garlic - 3 cloves, minced.
- Ginger - 1 tbsp, minced.
- Carrot - 1, grated.
- Bread crumbs - 1 cup.
- Egg - 1, beaten.
- Milk - 1/2 cup.
- Salt - to taste.
- Pepper - to taste.
- Oil - 2 tbsp.

Instructions

1. Preheat oven to 350°F (175°C).

2. Heat oil in a skillet over medium heat.

3. Sauté onions until golden brown.

4. Add garlic and ginger, and cook for 1-2 minutes.

5. Add ground beef and cook until browned.

6. Stir in grated carrot, salt, and pepper.

7. In a bowl, mix bread crumbs, beaten egg, and milk.

8. Add the beef mixture to the bread crumb mixture and mix well.

9. Transfer the mixture to a greased loaf pan and press down firmly.

10. Bake for 45-50 minutes until cooked through.

11. Let cool slightly before slicing and serving.

BEEF SUKUMA WIKI (BEEF WITH KALE)

Ingredients

- Beef - 1 lb, thinly sliced.
- Kale - 1 bunch, chopped.
- Onion - 1, sliced.
- Garlic - 3 cloves, minced.
- Tomato - 2, chopped.
- Salt - to taste.
- Pepper - to taste.
- Oil - 3 tbsp.

Instructions

1. Heat oil in a large skillet over medium heat.

2. Add sliced onions and cook until golden brown.

3. Add garlic and cook for 1-2 minutes.

4. Add sliced beef and cook until browned.

5. Stir in chopped tomatoes and cook until soft.

6. Add chopped kale and cook until wilted.

7. Season with salt and pepper.

8. Serve hot with ugali or rice.

BEEF AND POTATO CURRY

Ingredients

- Beef - 1 lb, cubed.
- Potatoes - 2, peeled and cubed.
- Onion - 1, finely chopped.
- Garlic - 3 cloves, minced.
- Ginger - 1 tbsp, minced.
- Tomato - 2, chopped.
- Coconut milk - 1 cup.
- Turmeric powder - 1 tsp.
- Cumin powder - 1 tsp.
- Coriander powder - 1 tsp.
- Salt - to taste.
- Pepper - to taste.
- Water - 2 cups.
- Oil - 2 tbsp.

Instructions

1. Heat oil in a pot over medium heat.

2. Sauté onions until golden brown.

3. Add garlic and ginger, and cook for 1-2 minutes.

4. Add beef cubes and brown on all sides.

5. Add chopped tomatoes and cook until soft.

6. Stir in turmeric, cumin, and coriander powders.

7. Add potatoes and mix well.

8. Pour in coconut milk and water, and bring to a boil.

9. Reduce heat and simmer until the beef and potatoes are tender.

10. Season with salt and pepper.

11. Serve hot with rice or chapati.

BEEF AND BANANA STEW

Ingredients

- Beef - 1 lb, cubed.
- Green bananas - 4, peeled and sliced.
- Onion - 1, finely chopped.
- Garlic - 3 cloves, minced.
- Ginger - 1 tbsp, minced.
- Tomato - 2, chopped.
- Carrot - 1, sliced.
- Water - 4 cups.
- Salt - to taste.
- Pepper - to taste.
- Oil - 2 tbsp.

Instructions

1. Heat oil in a pot over medium heat.

2. Sauté onions until golden brown.

3. Add garlic and ginger, and cook for 1-2 minutes.

4. Add beef cubes and brown on all sides.

5. Add chopped tomatoes and cook until soft.

6. Add sliced bananas and carrots, and mix well.

7. Pour in water and bring to a boil.

8. Reduce heat and simmer until the beef and bananas are tender.

9. Season with salt and pepper.

10. Serve hot with rice or chapati.

MSHIKAKI
(MARINATED BEEF SKEWERS)

Ingredients

- Beef - 1 lb, cubed.
- Lemon juice - 2 tbsp.
- Garlic - 4 cloves, minced.
- Ginger - 1 tbsp, minced.
- Salt - to taste.
- Pepper - to taste.
- Yogurt - 1/2 cup.
- Oil - for grilling.
- Skewers - as needed.

Instructions

1. In a bowl, mix lemon juice, garlic, ginger, salt, pepper, and yogurt.

2. Add beef cubes to the marinade and mix well.

3. Marinate for at least 2 hours or overnight in the refrigerator.

4. Preheat the grill to medium-high heat and brush with oil.

5. Thread the marinated beef onto skewers.

6. Grill the skewers until the beef is cooked through and charred, turning occasionally.

7. Serve hot with a side of kachumbari (tomato and onion salad).

UGALI NA NYAMA (CORNMEAL WITH MEAT)

Ingredients

- Cornmeal - 2 cups.
- Water - 4 cups.
- Beef - 1 lb, cubed.
- Onion - 1, finely chopped.
- Garlic - 3 cloves, minced.
- Ginger - 1 tbsp, minced.
- Tomato - 2, chopped.
- Carrot - 1, sliced.
- Salt - to taste.
- Pepper - to taste.
- Oil - 2 tbsp.

Instructions

1. Bring water to a boil in a pot.

2. Gradually add cornmeal, stirring continuously to avoid lumps.

3. Cook until the mixture thickens and pulls away from the sides of the pot.

4. Remove from heat and set aside.

5. Heat oil in another pot over medium heat.

6. Sauté onions until golden brown.

7. Add garlic and ginger, and cook for 1-2 minutes.

8. Add beef cubes and brown on all sides.

9. Add chopped tomatoes and cook until soft.

10. Add sliced carrots and mix well.

11. Pour in water and bring to a boil.

12. Reduce heat and simmer until the beef and vegetables are tender.

13. Season with salt and pepper.

14. Serve the meat stew hot with ugali.

BEEF AND EGGPLANT STEW

Ingredients

- Beef - 1 lb, cubed.
- Eggplant - 2, cubed.
- Onion - 1, finely chopped.
- Garlic - 3 cloves, minced.
- Ginger - 1 tbsp, minced.
- Tomato - 2, chopped.
- Coconut milk - 1 cup.

- Turmeric powder - 1 tsp.
- Cumin powder - 1 tsp.
- Coriander powder - 1 tsp.
- Salt - to taste.
- Pepper - to taste.
- Water - 2 cups.
- Oil - 2 tbsp.

Instructions

1. Heat oil in a pot over medium heat.

2. Sauté onions until golden brown.

3. Add garlic and ginger, and cook for 1-2 minutes.

4. Add beef cubes and brown on all sides.

5. Add chopped tomatoes and cook until soft.

6. Stir in turmeric, cumin, and coriander powders.

7. Add eggplant and mix well.

8. Pour in coconut milk and water, and bring to a boil.

9. Reduce heat and simmer until the beef and eggplant are tender.

10. Season with salt and pepper.

11. Serve hot with rice or chapati.

PORK DISHES

Tanzanian pork dishes are distinct for their flavorful depth and essential role within the local cuisine, offering a unique profile distinct from other meats. These dishes often feature pork combined with traditional spices and ingredients like garlic, ginger, and bell peppers, which not only boost the flavor but also augment the dish's nutritional profile. The preferred methods of preparation, such as braising or roasting, enhance the pork's natural tenderness and flavor while preserving its health benefits.

The adaptability of pork in Tanzanian recipes is evident in the array of dishes that cater to various tastes and dining contexts. From succulent pork skewers, known locally as mishkaki, to rich, hearty stews that simmer pork with vegetables and coconut milk, each dish celebrates the versatility of pork. This flexibility makes pork a favored choice in many households, fitting seamlessly into both everyday meals and special occasions.

Pork dishes in Tanzania are celebrated not just for their taste but also for their contribution to a balanced diet. They provide an excellent source of protein and essential vitamins, making them an integral part of nutritious eating in Tanzania.

KITIMOTO (FRIED PORK)

Ingredients

- Pork - 2 lbs, cut into pieces.
- Garlic - 4 cloves, minced.
- Ginger - 1 tbsp, minced.
- Lemon juice - 2 tbsp.

- Salt - to taste.
- Pepper - to taste.
- Oil - 2 tbsp.
- Onion - 1, sliced.
- Tomato - 2, chopped.
- Green chili - 1, chopped.

Instructions

1. In a bowl, mix garlic, ginger, lemon juice, salt, and pepper.

2. Add pork pieces to the marinade and mix well.

3. Marinate for at least 2 hours or overnight in the refrigerator.

4. Heat oil in a pot over medium heat.

5. Add marinated pork and cook until browned on all sides.

6. Add sliced onions, chopped tomatoes, and green chili.

7. Cook until the vegetables are soft and the pork is cooked through.

8. Serve hot with rice or chapati.

PORK RIBS

Ingredients

- Pork ribs - 2 lbs.
- Garlic - 4 cloves, minced.
- Ginger - 1 tbsp, minced.
- Honey - 2 tbsp.

- Soy sauce - 1/4 cup.
- Salt - to taste.
- Pepper - to taste.
- Oil - 2 tbsp.
- Onion - 1, sliced.

Instructions

1. In a bowl, mix garlic, ginger, honey, soy sauce, salt, and pepper.

2. Add pork ribs to the marinade and mix well.

3. Marinate for at least 2 hours or overnight in the refrigerator.

4. Preheat oven to 350°F (175°C).

5. Heat oil in a large skillet over medium heat.

6. Add marinated pork ribs and brown on all sides.

7. Transfer the ribs to a baking dish and cover with sliced onions.

8. Bake in the preheated oven for 1 hour or until the ribs are tender.

9. Serve hot with your favorite side dishes.

PORK STEW

Ingredients

- Pork - 1 lb, cubed.
- Onion - 1, chopped.
- Garlic - 3 cloves, minced.

- Ginger - 1 tbsp, minced.
- Tomato - 2, chopped.
- Potato - 2, cubed.
- Carrot - 1, sliced.
- Pork broth - 4 cups.
- Salt - to taste.
- Pepper - to taste.
- Oil - 3 tbsp.

Instructions

1. Heat oil in a pot over medium heat.

2. Add chopped onions and cook until golden brown.

3. Add garlic and ginger, and cook for 1-2 minutes.

4. Add pork cubes and brown on all sides.

5. Add chopped tomatoes, potatoes, and carrots.

6. Pour in pork broth and bring to a boil.

7. Reduce heat and simmer until the pork and vegetables are tender.

8. Season with salt and pepper.

9. Serve hot with rice or chapati.

CHOMA PORK (GRILLED PORK)

Ingredients

- Pork - 2 lbs, cut into pieces.
- Lemon juice - 2 tbsp.
- Garlic - 4 cloves, minced.

- Ginger - 1 tbsp, minced.
- Salt - to taste.
- Pepper - to taste.
- Oil - for grilling.

Instructions

1. In a bowl, mix lemon juice, garlic, ginger, salt, and pepper.

2. Add pork pieces to the marinade and mix well.

3. Marinate for at least 2 hours or overnight in the refrigerator.

4. Preheat the grill to medium-high heat and brush with oil.

5. Grill the pork until cooked through and charred, turning occasionally.

6. Serve hot with a side of kachumbari (tomato and onion salad).

PORK CURRY

Ingredients

- Pork - 1 lb, cubed.
- Onion - 1, finely chopped.
- Garlic - 3 cloves, minced.
- Ginger - 1 tbsp, minced.
- Tomato - 2, chopped.
- Coconut milk - 1 cup.
- Turmeric powder - 1 tsp.
- Cumin powder - 1 tsp.
- Coriander powder - 1 tsp.

- Salt - to taste.
- Pepper - to taste.
- Water - 2 cups.
- Oil - 2 tbsp.

Instructions

1. Heat oil in a pot over medium heat.

2. Sauté onions until golden brown.

3. Add garlic and ginger, and cook for 1-2 minutes.

4. Add pork cubes and brown on all sides.

5. Add chopped tomatoes and cook until soft.

6. Stir in turmeric, cumin, and coriander powders.

7. Pour in coconut milk and water, and bring to a boil.

8. Reduce heat and simmer until the pork is tender and the sauce thickens.

9. Season with salt and pepper.

10. Serve hot with rice or chapati.

PORK CHOPS

Ingredients

- Pork chops - 4.
- Garlic - 3 cloves, minced.
- Ginger - 1 tbsp, minced.
- Lemon juice - 2 tbsp.
- Soy sauce - 2 tbsp.

- Honey - 1 tbsp.
- Salt - to taste.
- Pepper - to taste.
- Oil - 2 tbsp.

Instructions

1. In a bowl, mix garlic, ginger, lemon juice, soy sauce, honey, salt, and pepper.

2. Add pork chops to the marinade and coat well.

3. Marinate for at least 1 hour or overnight in the refrigerator.

4. Heat oil in a skillet over medium heat.

5. Add pork chops and cook for 4-5 minutes on each side until golden brown and cooked through.

6. Serve hot with your favorite side dishes.

PORK AND BEAN CASSEROLE

Ingredients

- Pork - 1 lb, cubed.
- Kidney beans - 1 can, drained and rinsed.
- Onion - 1, chopped.
- Garlic - 3 cloves, minced.
- Tomato - 2, chopped.
- Carrot - 1, sliced.
- Celery - 2 stalks, chopped.
- Beef broth - 2 cups.
- Salt - to taste.
- Pepper - to taste.

- Oil - 2 tbsp.

Instructions

1. Preheat oven to 350°F (175°C).

2. Heat oil in a skillet over medium heat.

3. Sauté onions until golden brown.

4. Add garlic and cook for 1-2 minutes.

5. Add pork cubes and brown on all sides.

6. Add chopped tomatoes, carrots, and celery.

7. Stir in kidney beans and beef broth.

8. Season with salt and pepper.

9. Transfer the mixture to a baking dish and cover with foil.

10. Bake in the preheated oven for 1 hour or until the pork is tender.

11. Serve hot.

PORK PILAU

Ingredients

- Pork - 1 lb, cubed.
- Basmati rice - 2 cups.
- Onion - 1, chopped.
- Garlic - 3 cloves, minced.
- Ginger - 1 tbsp, minced.

- Tomato - 2, chopped.
- Carrot - 1, chopped.
- Potato - 2, cubed.
- Cumin seeds - 1 tsp.
- Cardamom pods - 4.
- Cinnamon stick - 1.
- Cloves - 4.
- Salt - to taste.
- Water - 4 cups.
- Oil - 3 tbsp.

Instructions

1. Heat oil in a large pot over medium heat.

2. Sauté onions until golden brown.

3. Add garlic, ginger, and whole spices (cumin, cardamom, cinnamon, cloves) and cook for 1-2 minutes.

4. Add pork cubes and brown on all sides.

5. Stir in chopped tomatoes, carrots, and potatoes.

6. Add rice and mix well.

7. Pour in water and bring to a boil.

8. Reduce heat, cover, and simmer until the rice is cooked and the liquid is absorbed.

9. Season with salt.

10. Serve hot.

SWEET AND SOUR PORK

Ingredients

- Pork - 1 lb, cubed.
- Pineapple chunks - 1 cup.
- Bell pepper - 1, chopped.
- Onion - 1, chopped.
- Garlic - 3 cloves, minced.
- Ginger - 1 tbsp, minced.
- Tomato ketchup - 1/4 cup.
- Vinegar - 2 tbsp.
- Soy sauce - 2 tbsp.
- Brown sugar - 2 tbsp.
- Cornstarch - 1 tbsp, mixed with 2 tbsp water.
- Salt - to taste.
- Pepper - to taste.
- Oil - 2 tbsp.

Instructions

1. Heat oil in a large skillet over medium heat.

2. Sauté onions until golden brown.

3. Add garlic and ginger, and cook for 1-2 minutes.

4. Add pork cubes and brown on all sides.

5. Stir in bell pepper and pineapple chunks.

6. In a bowl, mix tomato ketchup, vinegar, soy sauce, and brown sugar.

7. Pour the sauce into the skillet and mix well.

8. Add cornstarch mixture and stir until the sauce

thickens.

9. Season with salt and pepper.

10. Serve hot with rice.

SPICY PORK STIR FRY

Ingredients

- Pork - 1 lb, thinly sliced.
- Bell pepper - 1, sliced.
- Carrot - 1, julienned.
- Onion - 1, sliced.
- Garlic - 3 cloves, minced.
- Ginger - 1 tbsp, minced.
- Soy sauce - 2 tbsp.
- Chili sauce - 1 tbsp.
- Honey - 1 tbsp.
- Salt - to taste.
- Pepper - to taste.
- Oil - 2 tbsp.

Instructions

1. Heat oil in a large skillet or wok over medium-high heat.

2. Add garlic and ginger, and cook for 1-2 minutes.

3. Add sliced pork and stir-fry until browned.

4. Add bell pepper, carrot, and onion, and stir-fry for another 3-4 minutes.

5. In a bowl, mix soy sauce, chili sauce, and honey.

6. Pour the sauce into the skillet and mix well.

7. Stir-fry until the vegetables are tender and the pork is cooked through.

8. Season with salt and pepper.

9. Serve hot with rice or noodles.

PORK AND PINEAPPLE CURRY

Ingredients

- Pork - 1 lb, cubed.
- Pineapple chunks - 1 cup.
- Onion - 1, chopped.
- Garlic - 3 cloves, minced.
- Ginger - 1 tbsp, minced.
- Tomato - 2, chopped.
- Coconut milk - 1 cup.
- Turmeric powder - 1 tsp.
- Cumin powder - 1 tsp.
- Coriander powder - 1 tsp.
- Salt - to taste.
- Pepper - to taste.
- Oil - 2 tbsp.

Instructions

1. Heat oil in a pot over medium heat.

2. Sauté onions until golden brown.

3. Add garlic and ginger, and cook for 1-2 minutes.

4. Add pork cubes and brown on all sides.

5. Add chopped tomatoes and cook until soft.

6. Stir in turmeric, cumin, and coriander powders.

7. Add pineapple chunks and mix well.

8. Pour in coconut milk and bring to a boil.

9. Reduce heat and simmer until the pork is tender and the sauce thickens.

10. Season with salt and pepper.

11. Serve hot with rice or chapati.

PORK AND VEGETABLE KEBABS

Ingredients

- Pork - 1 lb, cubed.
- Bell pepper - 1, cut into chunks.
- Onion - 1, cut into chunks.
- Zucchini - 1, sliced.
- Garlic - 3 cloves, minced.
- Ginger - 1 tbsp, minced.
- Lemon juice - 2 tbsp.
- Soy sauce - 2 tbsp.
- Honey - 1 tbsp.
- Salt - to taste.
- Pepper - to taste.
- Oil - for grilling.
- Skewers - as needed.

Instructions

1. In a bowl, mix garlic, ginger, lemon juice, soy sauce, honey, salt, and pepper.

2. Add pork cubes to the marinade and coat well.

3. Marinate for at least 1 hour or overnight in the refrigerator.

4. Preheat the grill to medium-high heat and brush with oil.

5. Thread marinated pork, bell pepper, onion, and zucchini onto skewers.

6. Grill the kebabs until the pork is cooked through and the vegetables are tender, turning occasionally.

7. Serve hot with your favorite side dishes.

UGALI WITH PORK

Ingredients

- Cornmeal - 2 cups.
- Water - 4 cups.
- Pork - 1 lb, cubed.
- Onion - 1, chopped.
- Garlic - 3 cloves, minced.
- Ginger - 1 tbsp, minced.
- Tomato - 2, chopped.
- Carrot - 1, sliced.
- Salt - to taste.
- Pepper - to taste.
- Oil - 2 tbsp.

Instructions

1. Bring water to a boil in a pot.

2. Gradually add cornmeal, stirring continuously to avoid

lumps.

3. Cook until the mixture thickens and pulls away from the sides of the pot.

4. Remove from heat and set aside.

5. Heat oil in another pot over medium heat.

6. Sauté onions until golden brown.

7. Add garlic and ginger, and cook for 1-2 minutes.

8. Add pork cubes and brown on all sides.

9. Add chopped tomatoes and cook until soft.

10. Add sliced carrots and mix well.

11. Pour in water and bring to a boil.

12. Reduce heat and simmer until the pork and vegetables are tender.

13. Season with salt and pepper.

14. Serve the meat stew hot with ugali.

PORK MCHUZI

Ingredients

- Pork - 1 lb, cubed.
- Onion - 1, finely chopped.
- Garlic - 3 cloves, minced.
- Ginger - 1 tbsp, minced.
- Tomato - 2, chopped.

- Coconut milk - 1 cup.
- Turmeric powder - 1 tsp.
- Cumin powder - 1 tsp.
- Coriander powder - 1 tsp.
- Salt - to taste.
- Pepper - to taste.
- Water - 2 cups.
- Oil - 2 tbsp.

Instructions

1. Heat oil in a pot over medium heat.

2. Sauté onions until golden brown.

3. Add garlic and ginger, and cook for 1-2 minutes.

4. Add pork cubes and brown on all sides.

5. Add chopped tomatoes and cook until soft.

6. Stir in turmeric, cumin, and coriander powders.

7. Pour in coconut milk and water, and bring to a boil.

8. Reduce heat and simmer until the pork is tender and the sauce thickens.

9. Season with salt and pepper.

10. Serve hot with rice or chapati.

SMOKED PORK

Ingredients

- Pork - 2 lbs, cut into pieces.

- Garlic - 4 cloves, minced.
- Ginger - 1 tbsp, minced.
- Smoked paprika - 2 tsp.
- Soy sauce - 1/4 cup.
- Honey - 2 tbsp.
- Salt - to taste.
- Pepper - to taste.
- Oil - 2 tbsp.

Instructions

1. In a bowl, mix garlic, ginger, smoked paprika, soy sauce, honey, salt, and pepper.

2. Add pork pieces to the marinade and coat well.

3. Marinate for at least 2 hours or overnight in the refrigerator.

4. Preheat the grill or smoker to medium heat.

5. Smoke the pork until cooked through and tender, turning occasionally.

6. Serve hot with your favorite side dishes.

CHICKEN DISHES

Tanzanian chicken dishes are celebrated for their aromatic spices and diverse cooking techniques that distinctly differentiate them from other poultry dishes globally. These recipes often incorporate local ingredients like coconut, lime, and a variety of spices such as turmeric and coriander, enhancing the chicken's flavor and nutritional value. The methods of preparation, including grilling and stewing, ensure that the dishes are not only flavorful but also preserve the health benefits of the ingredients.

The versatility of chicken within Tanzanian cuisine is showcased through an array of dishes designed to suit different tastes and dietary needs. From the popular kuku paka, where chicken is cooked in a rich coconut sauce, to simpler, marinated grilled chicken skewers, each recipe offers a unique taste experience. This adaptability makes chicken a popular protein choice across various regions of Tanzania, enjoyed in both casual and formal dining settings.

Chicken dishes in Tanzania offer a nutritious alternative packed with protein and essential nutrients, vital for a balanced diet. They reflect the culinary diversity of the region, making them a staple in Tanzanian households and celebrations.

KUKU PAKA

Ingredients

- Chicken - 1 lb, cut into pieces.
- Onion - 1, finely chopped.

- Garlic - 3 cloves, minced.
- Ginger - 1 tbsp, minced.
- Tomato - 2, chopped.
- Coconut milk - 1 cup.
- Turmeric powder - 1 tsp.
- Cumin powder - 1 tsp.
- Coriander powder - 1 tsp.
- Salt - to taste.
- Pepper - to taste.
- Water - 1 cup.
- Oil - 2 tbsp.

Instructions

1. Heat oil in a pot over medium heat.

2. Sauté onions until golden brown.

3. Add garlic and ginger, and cook for 1-2 minutes.

4. Add chicken pieces and brown on all sides.

5. Add chopped tomatoes and cook until soft.

6. Stir in turmeric, cumin, and coriander powders.

7. Pour in coconut milk and water, and bring to a boil.

8. Reduce heat and simmer until the chicken is tender and the sauce thickens.

9. Season with salt and pepper.

10. Serve hot with rice or chapati.

KUKU CHOMA
(GRILLED CHICKEN)

Ingredients

- Chicken - 1 whole, cut into pieces.
- Lemon juice - 2 tbsp.
- Garlic - 4 cloves, minced.
- Ginger - 1 tbsp, minced.
- Paprika - 1 tsp.
- Turmeric powder - 1 tsp.
- Salt - to taste.
- Pepper - to taste.
- Oil - 2 tbsp.

Instructions

1. In a bowl, mix lemon juice, garlic, ginger, paprika, turmeric, salt, and pepper.

2. Add chicken pieces to the marinade and coat well.

3. Marinate for at least 2 hours or overnight in the refrigerator.

4. Preheat the grill to medium-high heat and brush with oil.

5. Grill the chicken until cooked through and charred, turning occasionally.

6. Serve hot with a side of kachumbari (tomato and onion salad).

CHICKEN PILAU

Ingredients

- Chicken - 1 lb, cut into pieces.
- Basmati rice - 2 cups.
- Onion - 1, chopped.
- Garlic - 3 cloves, minced.
- Ginger - 1 tbsp, minced.
- Tomato - 2, chopped.
- Carrot - 1, chopped.
- Potato - 2, cubed.
- Cumin seeds - 1 tsp.
- Cardamom pods - 4.
- Cinnamon stick - 1.
- Cloves - 4.
- Salt - to taste.
- Water - 4 cups.
- Oil - 3 tbsp.

Instructions

1. Heat oil in a large pot over medium heat.

2. Sauté onions until golden brown.

3. Add garlic, ginger, and whole spices (cumin, cardamom, cinnamon, cloves) and cook for 1-2 minutes.

4. Add chicken pieces and brown on all sides.

5. Stir in chopped tomatoes, carrots, and potatoes.

6. Add rice and mix well.

7. Pour in water and bring to a boil.

8. Reduce heat, cover, and simmer until the rice is cooked and the liquid is absorbed.

9. Season with salt.

10. Serve hot.

CHICKEN BIRYANI

Ingredients

- Chicken - 1 lb, cut into pieces.
- Basmati rice - 2 cups.
- Onion - 1, finely chopped.
- Garlic - 3 cloves, minced.
- Ginger - 1 tbsp, minced.
- Tomato - 2, chopped.
- Yogurt - 1 cup.
- Mint leaves - 1/4 cup, chopped.
- Cilantro - 1/4 cup, chopped.
- Cumin powder - 1 tsp.
- Coriander powder - 1 tsp.
- Turmeric powder - 1/2 tsp.
- Salt - to taste.
- Water - 4 cups.
- Oil - 3 tbsp.

Instructions

1. Heat oil in a large pot over medium heat.

2. Sauté onions until golden brown.

3. Add garlic, ginger, cumin, coriander, and turmeric powders and cook for 1-2 minutes.

4. Add chicken pieces and brown on all sides.

5. Stir in chopped tomatoes and yogurt.

6. Add mint leaves and cilantro.

7. Add rice and mix well.

8. Pour in water and bring to a boil.

9. Reduce heat, cover, and simmer until the rice is cooked and the liquid is absorbed.

10. Season with salt. Serve hot.

KUKU NA NAZI
(CHICKEN IN COCONUT SAUCE)

Ingredients

- Chicken - 1 lb, cut into pieces.
- Onion - 1, finely chopped.
- Garlic - 3 cloves, minced.
- Ginger - 1 tbsp, minced.
- Tomato - 2, chopped.
- Coconut milk - 1 cup.
- Turmeric powder - 1 tsp.
- Cumin powder - 1 tsp.
- Coriander powder - 1 tsp.
- Salt - to taste.
- Pepper - to taste.
- Water - 1 cup.
- Oil - 2 tbsp.

Instructions

1. Heat oil in a pot over medium heat.

2. Sauté onions until golden brown.

3. Add garlic and ginger, and cook for 1-2 minutes.

4. Add chicken pieces and brown on all sides.

5. Add chopped tomatoes and cook until soft.

6. Stir in turmeric, cumin, and coriander powders.

7. Pour in coconut milk and water, and bring to a boil.

8. Reduce heat and simmer until the chicken is tender and the sauce thickens.

9. Season with salt and pepper.

10. Serve hot with rice or chapati.

CHICKEN STEW

Ingredients

- Chicken - 1 lb, cut into pieces.
- Onion - 1, chopped.
- Garlic - 3 cloves, minced.
- Ginger - 1 tbsp, minced.
- Tomato - 2, chopped.
- Potato - 2, cubed.
- Carrot - 1, sliced.
- Chicken broth - 4 cups.
- Salt - to taste.
- Pepper - to taste.
- Oil - 2 tbsp.

Instructions

1. Heat oil in a pot over medium heat.

2. Sauté onions until golden brown.

3. Add garlic and ginger, and cook for 1-2 minutes.

4. Add chicken pieces and brown on all sides.

5. Add chopped tomatoes, potatoes, and carrots.

6. Pour in chicken broth and bring to a boil.

7. Reduce heat and simmer until the chicken and vegetables are tender.

8. Season with salt and pepper.

9. Serve hot with rice or chapati.

CHICKEN AND VEGETABLE STIR FRY

Ingredients

- Chicken - 1 lb, thinly sliced.
- Bell pepper - 1, sliced.
- Carrot - 1, julienned.
- Onion - 1, sliced.
- Garlic - 3 cloves, minced.
- Ginger - 1 tbsp, minced.
- Soy sauce - 2 tbsp.
- Chili sauce - 1 tbsp.
- Honey - 1 tbsp.
- Salt - to taste.
- Pepper - to taste.
- Oil - 2 tbsp.

Instructions

1. Heat oil in a large skillet or wok over medium-high

heat.

2. Add garlic and ginger, and cook for 1-2 minutes.

3. Add sliced chicken and stir-fry until browned.

4. Add bell pepper, carrot, and onion, and stir-fry for another 3-4 minutes.

5. In a bowl, mix soy sauce, chili sauce, and honey.

6. Pour the sauce into the skillet and mix well.

7. Stir-fry until the vegetables are tender and the chicken is cooked through.

8. Season with salt and pepper.

9. Serve hot with rice or noodles.

CHICKEN AND PEANUT STEW

Ingredients

- Chicken - 1 lb, cut into pieces.
- Peanut butter - 1/2 cup.
- Onion - 1, chopped.
- Garlic - 3 cloves, minced.
- Ginger - 1 tbsp, minced.
- Tomato - 2, chopped.
- Carrot - 1, sliced.
- Chicken broth - 4 cups.
- Salt - to taste.
- Pepper - to taste.
- Oil - 2 tbsp.

Instructions

1. Heat oil in a pot over medium heat.

2. Sauté onions until golden brown.

3. Add garlic and ginger, and cook for 1-2 minutes.

4. Add chicken pieces and brown on all sides.

5. Add chopped tomatoes and cook until soft.

6. Stir in peanut butter and mix well.

7. Add sliced carrots and pour in chicken broth.

8. Bring to a boil, then reduce heat and simmer until the chicken and vegetables are tender.

9. Season with salt and pepper.

10. Serve hot with rice or chapati.

FRIED CHICKEN

Ingredients

- Chicken - 1 lb, cut into pieces.
- Flour - 1 cup.
- Garlic powder - 1 tsp.
- Onion powder - 1 tsp.
- Paprika - 1 tsp.
- Salt - to taste.
- Pepper - to taste.
- Egg - 1, beaten.
- Milk - 1/2 cup.
- Oil - for frying.

Instructions

1. In a bowl, mix flour, garlic powder, onion powder, paprika, salt, and pepper.

2. In another bowl, mix beaten egg and milk.

3. Dip chicken pieces in the egg mixture, then coat with the flour mixture.

4. Heat oil in a large skillet over medium heat.

5. Fry the chicken pieces until golden brown and cooked through, turning occasionally.

6. Drain on paper towels.

7. Serve hot with your favorite side dishes.

CHICKEN SUKUMA WIKI

Ingredients

- Chicken - 1 lb, cut into pieces.
- Kale - 1 bunch, chopped.
- Onion - 1, sliced.
- Garlic - 3 cloves, minced.
- Tomato - 2, chopped.
- Salt - to taste.
- Pepper - to taste.
- Oil - 2 tbsp.

Instructions

1. Heat oil in a large skillet over medium heat.

2. Add sliced onions and cook until golden brown.

3. Add garlic and cook for 1-2 minutes.

4. Add chicken pieces and cook until browned.

5. Stir in chopped tomatoes and cook until soft.

6. Add chopped kale and cook until wilted.

7. Season with salt and pepper.

8. Serve hot with ugali or rice.

CHICKEN AND POTATO CURRY

Ingredients

- Chicken - 1 lb, cut into pieces.
- Potatoes - 2, peeled and cubed.
- Onion - 1, chopped.
- Garlic - 3 cloves, minced.
- Ginger - 1 tbsp, minced.
- Tomato - 2, chopped.
- Coconut milk - 1 cup.
- Turmeric powder - 1 tsp.
- Cumin powder - 1 tsp.
- Coriander powder - 1 tsp.
- Salt - to taste.
- Pepper - to taste.
- Water - 2 cups.
- Oil - 2 tbsp.

Instructions

1. Heat oil in a pot over medium heat.

2. Sauté onions until golden brown.

3. Add garlic and ginger, and cook for 1-2 minutes.

4. Add chicken pieces and brown on all sides.

5. Add chopped tomatoes and cook until soft.

6. Stir in turmeric, cumin, and coriander powders.

7. Add potatoes and mix well.

8. Pour in coconut milk and water, and bring to a boil.

9. Reduce heat and simmer until the chicken and potatoes are tender.

10. Season with salt and pepper.

11. Serve hot with rice or chapati.

SPICED CHICKEN WINGS

Ingredients

- Chicken wings - 2 lbs.
- Garlic - 4 cloves, minced.
- Ginger - 1 tbsp, minced.
- Paprika - 1 tsp.
- Cumin powder - 1 tsp.
- Chili powder - 1 tsp.
- Turmeric powder - 1/2 tsp.
- Salt - to taste.
- Pepper - to taste.
- Oil - 2 tbsp.

Instructions

1. In a bowl, mix garlic, ginger, paprika, cumin, chili

powder, turmeric, salt, and pepper.

2. Add chicken wings to the spice mixture and coat well.

3. Marinate for at least 1 hour or overnight in the refrigerator.

4. Preheat the oven to 400°F (200°C).

5. Arrange the chicken wings on a baking sheet and drizzle with oil.

6. Bake for 25-30 minutes, turning halfway through, until golden brown and crispy.

7. Serve hot with your favorite dipping sauce.

CHICKEN AND RICE CASSEROLE

Ingredients

- Chicken - 1 lb, cut into pieces.
- Basmati rice - 2 cups.
- Onion - 1, chopped.
- Garlic - 3 cloves, minced.
- Ginger - 1 tbsp, minced.
- Tomato - 2, chopped.
- Carrot - 1, chopped.
- Green peas - 1 cup.
- Chicken broth - 4 cups.
- Salt - to taste.
- Pepper - to taste.
- Oil - 2 tbsp.

Instructions

1. Preheat oven to 350°F (175°C).

2. Heat oil in a skillet over medium heat.

3. Sauté onions until golden brown.

4. Add garlic and ginger, and cook for 1-2 minutes.

5. Add chicken pieces and brown on all sides.

6. Stir in chopped tomatoes, carrots, and green peas.

7. Add rice and mix well.

8. Pour in chicken broth and bring to a boil.

9. Transfer the mixture to a baking dish and cover with foil.

10. Bake in the preheated oven for 30-35 minutes, until the rice is cooked and the liquid is absorbed.

11. Season with salt and pepper.

12. Serve hot.

CHICKEN KEBABS

Ingredients

- Chicken - 1 lb, cubed.
- Bell pepper - 1, cut into chunks.
- Onion - 1, cut into chunks.
- Zucchini - 1, sliced.
- Garlic - 3 cloves, minced.
- Ginger - 1 tbsp, minced.
- Lemon juice - 2 tbsp.
- Soy sauce - 2 tbsp.
- Honey - 1 tbsp.

- Salt - to taste.
- Pepper - to taste.
- Oil - for grilling.
- Skewers - as needed.

Instructions

1. In a bowl, mix garlic, ginger, lemon juice, soy sauce, honey, salt, and pepper.

2. Add chicken cubes to the marinade and coat well.

3. Marinate for at least 1 hour or overnight in the refrigerator.

4. Preheat the grill to medium-high heat and brush with oil.

5. Thread marinated chicken, bell pepper, onion, and zucchini onto skewers.

6. Grill the kebabs until the chicken is cooked through and the vegetables are tender, turning occasionally.

7. Serve hot with your favorite side dishes.

CHICKEN AND PLANTAIN CURRY

Ingredients

- Chicken - 1 lb, cut into pieces.
- Plantains - 2, peeled and sliced.
- Onion - 1, chopped.
- Garlic - 3 cloves, minced.
- Ginger - 1 tbsp, minced.
- Tomato - 2, chopped.
- Coconut milk - 1 cup.

- Turmeric powder - 1 tsp.
- Cumin powder - 1 tsp.
- Coriander powder - 1 tsp.
- Salt - to taste.
- Pepper - to taste.
- Water - 2 cups.
- Oil - 2 tbsp.

Instructions

1. Heat oil in a pot over medium heat.

2. Sauté onions until golden brown.

3. Add garlic and ginger, and cook for 1-2 minutes.

4. Add chicken pieces and brown on all sides.

5. Add chopped tomatoes and cook until soft.

6. Stir in turmeric, cumin, and coriander powders.

7. Add plantains and mix well.

8. Pour in coconut milk and water, and bring to a boil.

9. Reduce heat and simmer until the chicken and plantains are tender.

10. Season with salt and pepper.

11. Serve hot with rice or chapati.

GOAT DISHES

Tanzanian goat dishes are renowned for their robust flavors and nutritional benefits, setting them apart from other types of meat commonly found in the region. These dishes often utilize goat meat marinated in an array of local spices, including garlic, chili, and cumin, which not only tenderize the meat but also infuse it with rich, savory notes. The cooking techniques, such as slow simmering and roasting, ensure that the meat is both flavorful and tender, maximizing its health benefits by retaining essential nutrients.

The adaptability of goat meat in Tanzanian recipes is evident in the diverse ways it is prepared and served. From hearty stews that simmer goat meat with vegetables to skewered and grilled pieces known as mishkaki, goat dishes are a culinary delight. This versatility allows it to be a favorite in both everyday meals and festive occasions, catering to a variety of tastes and preferences.

Goat meat is a nutritional powerhouse, offering a leaner alternative to other red meats, rich in protein and low in cholesterol. Its role in Tanzanian cuisine underscores a commitment to health-conscious eating, highlighting its value in a balanced diet.

MBUZI CHOMA (ROASTED GOAT)

Ingredients

- Goat meat - 2 lbs, cut into pieces.
- Lemon juice - 2 tbsp.
- Garlic - 4 cloves, minced.
- Ginger - 1 tbsp, minced.
- Salt - to taste.

- Pepper - to taste.
- Oil - 2 tbsp.

Instructions

1. In a bowl, mix lemon juice, garlic, ginger, salt, and pepper.

2. Add goat pieces to the marinade and mix well.

3. Marinate for at least 2 hours or overnight in the refrigerator.

4. Preheat the grill to medium-high heat and brush with oil.

5. Grill the goat until cooked through and charred, turning occasionally.

6. Serve hot with a side of kachumbari (tomato and onion salad).

GOAT CURRY

Ingredients

- Goat meat - 1 lb, cubed.
- Onion - 1, finely chopped.
- Garlic - 3 cloves, minced.
- Ginger - 1 tbsp, minced.
- Tomato - 2, chopped.
- Coconut milk - 1 cup.
- Turmeric powder - 1 tsp.
- Cumin powder - 1 tsp.
- Coriander powder - 1 tsp.
- Salt - to taste.
- Pepper - to taste.

- Water - 2 cups.
- Oil - 2 tbsp.

Instructions

1. Heat oil in a pot over medium heat.

2. Sauté onions until golden brown.

3. Add garlic and ginger, and cook for 1-2 minutes.

4. Add goat pieces and brown on all sides.

5. Add chopped tomatoes and cook until soft.

6. Stir in turmeric, cumin, and coriander powders.

7. Pour in coconut milk and water, and bring to a boil.

8. Reduce heat and simmer until the goat is tender and the sauce thickens.

9. Season with salt and pepper.

10. Serve hot with rice or chapati.

GOAT PILAU

Ingredients

- Goat meat - 1 lb, cubed.
- Basmati rice - 2 cups.
- Onion - 1, chopped.
- Garlic - 3 cloves, minced.
- Ginger - 1 tbsp, minced.
- Tomato - 2, chopped.
- Carrot - 1, chopped.

- Potato - 2, cubed.
- Cumin seeds - 1 tsp.
- Cardamom pods - 4.
- Cinnamon stick - 1.
- Cloves - 4.
- Salt - to taste.
- Water - 4 cups.
- Oil - 3 tbsp.

Instructions

1. Heat oil in a large pot over medium heat.

2. Sauté onions until golden brown.

3. Add garlic, ginger, and whole spices (cumin, cardamom, cinnamon, cloves) and cook for 1-2 minutes.

4. Add goat pieces and brown on all sides.

5. Stir in chopped tomatoes, carrots, and potatoes.

6. Add rice and mix well.

7. Pour in water and bring to a boil.

8. Reduce heat, cover, and simmer until the rice is cooked and the liquid is absorbed.

9. Season with salt.

10. Serve hot.

GOAT BIRYANI

Ingredients

- Goat meat - 1 lb, cubed.
- Basmati rice - 2 cups.
- Onion - 1, finely chopped.
- Garlic - 3 cloves, minced.
- Ginger - 1 tbsp, minced.
- Tomato - 2, chopped.
- Yogurt - 1 cup.
- Mint leaves - 1/4 cup, chopped.
- Cilantro - 1/4 cup, chopped.
- Cumin powder - 1 tsp.
- Coriander powder - 1 tsp.
- Turmeric powder - 1/2 tsp.
- Salt - to taste.
- Water - 4 cups.
- Oil - 3 tbsp.

Instructions

1. Heat oil in a large pot over medium heat.

2. Sauté onions until golden brown.

3. Add garlic, ginger, cumin, coriander, and turmeric powders and cook for 1-2 minutes.

4. Add goat pieces and brown on all sides.

5. Stir in chopped tomatoes and yogurt.

6. Add mint leaves and cilantro.

7. Add rice and mix well.

8. Pour in water and bring to a boil.

9. Reduce heat, cover, and simmer until the rice is cooked and the liquid is absorbed.

10. Season with salt.

11. Serve hot.

GOAT STEW

Ingredients

- Goat meat - 1 lb, cubed.
- Onion - 1, chopped.
- Garlic - 3 cloves, minced.
- Ginger - 1 tbsp, minced.
- Tomato - 2, chopped.
- Potato - 2, cubed.
- Carrot - 1, sliced.
- Goat broth - 4 cups.
- Salt - to taste.
- Pepper - to taste.
- Oil - 3 tbsp.

Instructions

1. Heat oil in a pot over medium heat.

2. Sauté onions until golden brown.

3. Add garlic and ginger, and cook for 1-2 minutes.

4. Add goat pieces and brown on all sides.

5. Add chopped tomatoes, potatoes, and carrots.

6. Pour in goat broth and bring to a boil.

7. Reduce heat and simmer until the goat and vegetables are tender.

8. Season with salt and pepper.

9. Serve hot with rice or chapati.

FRIED GOAT

Ingredients

- Goat meat - 1 lb, thinly sliced.
- Onion - 1, sliced.
- Garlic - 3 cloves, minced.
- Ginger - 1 tbsp, minced.
- Green bell pepper - 1, sliced.
- Tomato - 2, chopped.
- Soy sauce - 2 tbsp.
- Salt - to taste.
- Pepper - to taste.
- Oil - 3 tbsp.

Instructions

1. Heat oil in a large skillet over medium heat.

2. Add sliced onions and cook until golden brown.

3. Add garlic and ginger, and cook for 1-2 minutes.

4. Add sliced goat meat and stir-fry until browned.

5. Add green bell pepper and cook for another 2-3 minutes.

6. Stir in chopped tomatoes and soy sauce.

7. Cook until the goat is tender and the vegetables are soft.

8. Season with salt and pepper.

9. Serve hot with rice or chapati.

GOAT AND VEGETABLE STIR FRY

Ingredients

- Goat meat - 1 lb, thinly sliced.
- Bell pepper - 1, sliced.
- Carrot - 1, julienned.
- Onion - 1, sliced.
- Garlic - 3 cloves, minced.
- Ginger - 1 tbsp, minced.
- Soy sauce - 2 tbsp.
- Chili sauce - 1 tbsp.
- Honey - 1 tbsp.
- Salt - to taste.
- Pepper - to taste.
- Oil - 2 tbsp.

Instructions

1. Heat oil in a large skillet or wok over medium-high heat.

2. Add garlic and ginger, and cook for 1-2 minutes.

3. Add sliced goat meat and stir-fry until browned.

4. Add bell pepper, carrot, and onion, and stir-fry for another 3-4 minutes.

5. In a bowl, mix soy sauce, chili sauce, and honey.

6. Pour the sauce into the skillet and mix well.

7. Stir-fry until the vegetables are tender and the goat is cooked through.

8. Season with salt and pepper.

9. Serve hot with rice or noodles.

GOAT AND PEANUT STEW

Ingredients

- Goat meat - 1 lb, cut into pieces.
- Peanut butter - 1/2 cup.
- Onion - 1, chopped.
- Garlic - 3 cloves, minced.
- Ginger - 1 tbsp, minced.
- Tomato - 2, chopped.
- Carrot - 1, sliced.
- Goat broth - 4 cups.
- Salt - to taste.
- Pepper - to taste.
- Oil - 2 tbsp.

Instructions

1. Heat oil in a pot over medium heat.

2. Sauté onions until golden brown.

3. Add garlic and ginger, and cook for 1-2 minutes.

4. Add goat pieces and brown on all sides.

5. Add chopped tomatoes and cook until soft.

6. Stir in peanut butter and mix well.

7. Add sliced carrots and pour in goat broth.

8. Bring to a boil, then reduce heat and simmer until the goat and vegetables are tender.

9. Season with salt and pepper.

10. Serve hot with rice or chapati.

GOAT KEBABS

Ingredients

- Goat meat - 1 lb, cubed.
- Bell pepper - 1, cut into chunks.
- Onion - 1, cut into chunks.
- Zucchini - 1, sliced.
- Garlic - 3 cloves, minced.
- Ginger - 1 tbsp, minced.
- Lemon juice - 2 tbsp.
- Soy sauce - 2 tbsp.
- Honey - 1 tbsp.
- Salt - to taste.
- Pepper - to taste.
- Oil - for grilling.
- Skewers - as needed.

Instructions

1. In a bowl, mix garlic, ginger, lemon juice, soy sauce, honey, salt, and pepper.

2. Add goat cubes to the marinade and coat well.

3. Marinate for at least 1 hour or overnight in the refrigerator.

4. Preheat the grill to medium-high heat and brush with oil.

5. Thread marinated goat, bell pepper, onion, and zucchini onto skewers.

6. Grill the kebabs until the goat is cooked through and the vegetables are tender, turning occasionally.

7. Serve hot with your favorite side dishes.

GOAT AND BANANA CURRY

Ingredients

- Goat meat - 1 lb, cut into pieces.
- Green bananas - 4, peeled and sliced.
- Onion - 1, chopped.
- Garlic - 3 cloves, minced.
- Ginger - 1 tbsp, minced.
- Tomato - 2, chopped.
- Coconut milk - 1 cup.
- Turmeric powder - 1 tsp.
- Cumin powder - 1 tsp.
- Coriander powder - 1 tsp.
- Salt - to taste.
- Pepper - to taste.
- Water - 2 cups.
- Oil - 2 tbsp.

Instructions

1. Heat oil in a pot over medium heat.

2. Sauté onions until golden brown.

3. Add garlic and ginger, and cook for 1-2 minutes.

4. Add goat pieces and brown on all sides.

5. Add chopped tomatoes and cook until soft.

6. Stir in turmeric, cumin, and coriander powders.

7. Add sliced bananas and mix well.

8. Pour in coconut milk and water, and bring to a boil.

9. Reduce heat and simmer until the goat and bananas are tender.

10. Season with salt and pepper.

11. Serve hot with rice or chapati.

SPICED GOAT

Ingredients

- Goat meat - 1 lb, cubed.
- Garlic - 4 cloves, minced.
- Ginger - 1 tbsp, minced.
- Paprika - 1 tsp.
- Cumin powder - 1 tsp.
- Chili powder - 1 tsp.
- Turmeric powder - 1/2 tsp.
- Salt - to taste.
- Pepper - to taste.
- Oil - 2 tbsp.

Instructions

1. In a bowl, mix garlic, ginger, paprika, cumin, chili powder, turmeric, salt, and pepper.

2. Add goat cubes to the spice mixture and coat well.

3. Marinate for at least 1 hour or overnight in the refrigerator.

4. Heat oil in a large skillet over medium heat.

5. Add marinated goat and cook until browned and cooked through.

6. Serve hot with your favorite side dishes.

GOAT AND RICE CASSEROLE

Ingredients

- Goat meat - 1 lb, cubed.
- Basmati rice - 2 cups.
- Onion - 1, chopped.
- Garlic - 3 cloves, minced.
- Ginger - 1 tbsp, minced.
- Tomato - 2, chopped.
- Carrot - 1, chopped.
- Green peas - 1 cup.
- Goat broth - 4 cups.
- Salt - to taste.
- Pepper - to taste.
- Oil - 2 tbsp.

Instructions

1. Preheat oven to 350°F (175°C).

2. Heat oil in a skillet over medium heat.

3. Sauté onions until golden brown.

4. Add garlic and ginger, and cook for 1-2 minutes.

5. Add goat pieces and brown on all sides.

6. Stir in chopped tomatoes, carrots, and green peas.

7. Add rice and mix well.

8. Pour in goat broth and bring to a boil.

9. Transfer the mixture to a baking dish and cover with foil.

10. Bake in the preheated oven for 30-35 minutes, until the rice is cooked and the liquid is absorbed.

11. Season with salt and pepper.

12. Serve hot.

GOAT SUKUMA WIKI

Ingredients

- Goat meat - 1 lb, cut into pieces.
- Kale - 1 bunch, chopped.
- Onion - 1, sliced.
- Garlic - 3 cloves, minced.
- Tomato - 2, chopped.
- Salt - to taste.
- Pepper - to taste.
- Oil - 2 tbsp.

Instructions

1. Heat oil in a large skillet over medium heat.

2. Add sliced onions and cook until golden brown.

3. Add garlic and cook for 1-2 minutes.

4. Add goat pieces and cook until browned.

5. Stir in chopped tomatoes and cook until soft.

6. Add chopped kale and cook until wilted.

7. Season with salt and pepper.

8. Serve hot with ugali or rice.

GOAT AND POTATO STEW

Ingredients

- Goat meat - 1 lb, cubed.
- Potatoes - 2, peeled and cubed.
- Onion - 1, chopped.
- Garlic - 3 cloves, minced.
- Ginger - 1 tbsp, minced.
- Tomato - 2, chopped.
- Goat broth - 4 cups.
- Salt - to taste.
- Pepper - to taste.
- Oil - 2 tbsp.

Instructions

1. Heat oil in a pot over medium heat.

2. Sauté onions until golden brown.

3. Add garlic and ginger, and cook for 1-2 minutes.

4. Add goat pieces and brown on all sides.

5. Add chopped tomatoes and cook until soft.

6. Add potatoes and mix well.

7. Pour in goat broth and bring to a boil.

8. Reduce heat and simmer until the goat and potatoes are tender.

9. Season with salt and pepper.

10. Serve hot with rice or chapati.

SMOKED GOAT

Ingredients

- Goat meat - 2 lbs, cut into pieces.
- Garlic - 4 cloves, minced.
- Ginger - 1 tbsp, minced.
- Smoked paprika - 2 tsp.
- Soy sauce - 1/4 cup.
- Honey - 2 tbsp.
- Salt - to taste.
- Pepper - to taste.
- Oil - 2 tbsp.

Instructions

1. In a bowl, mix garlic, ginger, smoked paprika, soy sauce, honey, salt, and pepper.

2. Add goat pieces to the marinade and coat well.

3. Marinate for at least 2 hours or overnight in the refrigerator.

4. Preheat the grill or smoker to medium heat.

5. Smoke the goat until cooked through and tender, turning occasionally.

6. Serve hot with your favorite side dishes.

SEAFOOD DISHES

Tanzanian seafood dishes are celebrated for their freshness and the rich variety sourced from the Indian Ocean, distinguishing them sharply from inland culinary traditions. These dishes often feature fish, prawns, and octopus, seasoned with a unique blend of spices such as coconut, tamarind, and curry leaves, enhancing both flavor and nutritional content. The preparation methods, whether grilled, stewed, or curried, not only preserve the delicate textures and flavors of the seafood but also its health benefits.

The versatility of seafood in Tanzanian cuisine is reflected in the variety of dishes that appeal to different palates and dietary needs. From piquant fish curries to grilled prawns and fried octopus, each dish offers a distinct taste of the coastal regions' culinary heritage. This adaptability makes seafood a cornerstone of both everyday and celebratory meals, aligning with both local tastes and health-conscious choices.

Seafood dishes in Tanzania provide a rich source of protein and omega-3 fatty acids, essential for a balanced diet. Their prominence in the Tanzanian diet underscores an enduring appreciation for both the culinary and nutritional value of the ocean's bounty.

SAMAKI WA KUPAKA
(GRILLED FISH WITH COCONUT)

Ingredients

- Fish - 1 whole, cleaned and scaled.
- Coconut milk - 1 cup.
- Garlic - 3 cloves, minced.

- Ginger - 1 tbsp, minced.
- Turmeric powder - 1 tsp.
- Chili powder - 1 tsp.
- Salt - to taste.
- Pepper - to taste.
- Lemon juice - 2 tbsp.
- Oil - 2 tbsp.

Instructions

1. In a bowl, mix coconut milk, garlic, ginger, turmeric, chili powder, salt, pepper, and lemon juice.

2. Marinate the fish in the mixture for at least 1 hour.

3. Preheat the grill to medium heat and brush with oil.

4. Grill the fish, basting with the marinade, until cooked through and slightly charred.

5. Serve hot with a side of coconut rice or chapati.

MCHUZI WA SAMAKI (FISH CURRY)

Ingredients

- Fish fillets - 1 lb, cut into pieces.
- Onion - 1, chopped.
- Garlic - 3 cloves, minced.
- Ginger - 1 tbsp, minced.
- Tomato - 2, chopped.
- Coconut milk - 1 cup.
- Turmeric powder - 1 tsp.
- Cumin powder - 1 tsp.
- Coriander powder - 1 tsp.
- Salt - to taste.
- Pepper - to taste.

- Water - 2 cups.
- Oil - 2 tbsp.

Instructions

1. Heat oil in a pot over medium heat.

2. Sauté onions until golden brown.

3. Add garlic and ginger, and cook for 1-2 minutes.

4. Add fish pieces and brown on all sides.

5. Add chopped tomatoes and cook until soft.

6. Stir in turmeric, cumin, and coriander powders.

7. Pour in coconut milk and water, and bring to a boil.

8. Reduce heat and simmer until the fish is tender and the sauce thickens.

9. Season with salt and pepper.

10. Serve hot with rice or chapati.

GRILLED PRAWNS

Ingredients

- Prawns - 1 lb, cleaned and deveined.
- Garlic - 3 cloves, minced.
- Ginger - 1 tbsp, minced.
- Lemon juice - 2 tbsp.
- Chili powder - 1 tsp.
- Salt - to taste.
- Pepper - to taste.

- Oil - 2 tbsp.

Instructions

1. In a bowl, mix garlic, ginger, lemon juice, chili powder, salt, and pepper.

2. Marinate the prawns in the mixture for at least 30 minutes.

3. Preheat the grill to medium-high heat and brush with oil.

4. Grill the prawns until pink and cooked through, turning occasionally.

5. Serve hot with a side of lemon wedges and a fresh salad.

FISH BIRYANI

Ingredients

- Fish fillets - 1 lb, cut into pieces.
- Basmati rice - 2 cups.
- Onion - 1, finely chopped.
- Garlic - 3 cloves, minced.
- Ginger - 1 tbsp, minced.
- Tomato - 2, chopped.
- Yogurt - 1 cup.
- Mint leaves - 1/4 cup, chopped.
- Cilantro - 1/4 cup, chopped.
- Cumin powder - 1 tsp.
- Coriander powder - 1 tsp.
- Turmeric powder - 1/2 tsp.
- Salt - to taste.
- Water - 4 cups.

- Oil - 3 tbsp.

Instructions

1. Heat oil in a large pot over medium heat.

2. Sauté onions until golden brown.

3. Add garlic, ginger, cumin, coriander, and turmeric powders and cook for 1-2 minutes.

4. Add fish pieces and brown on all sides.

5. Stir in chopped tomatoes and yogurt.

6. Add mint leaves and cilantro.

7. Add rice and mix well.

8. Pour in water and bring to a boil.

9. Reduce heat, cover, and simmer until the rice is cooked and the liquid is absorbed.

10. Season with salt.

11. Serve hot.

FISH PILAU

Ingredients

- Fish fillets - 1 lb, cut into pieces.
- Basmati rice - 2 cups.
- Onion - 1, chopped.
- Garlic - 3 cloves, minced.
- Ginger - 1 tbsp, minced.

- Tomato - 2, chopped.
- Carrot - 1, chopped.
- Potato - 2, cubed.
- Cumin seeds - 1 tsp.
- Cardamom pods - 4.
- Cinnamon stick - 1.
- Cloves - 4.
- Salt - to taste.
- Water - 4 cups.
- Oil - 3 tbsp.

Instructions

1. Heat oil in a large pot over medium heat.

2. Sauté onions until golden brown.

3. Add garlic, ginger, and whole spices (cumin, cardamom, cinnamon, cloves) and cook for 1-2 minutes.

4. Add fish pieces and brown on all sides.

5. Stir in chopped tomatoes, carrots, and potatoes.

6. Add rice and mix well.

7. Pour in water and bring to a boil.

8. Reduce heat, cover, and simmer until the rice is cooked and the liquid is absorbed.

9. Season with salt.

10. Serve hot.

OCTOPUS CURRY

Ingredients

- Octopus - 1 lb, cleaned and cut into pieces.
- Onion - 1, finely chopped.
- Garlic - 3 cloves, minced.
- Ginger - 1 tbsp, minced.
- Tomato - 2, chopped.
- Coconut milk - 1 cup.
- Turmeric powder - 1 tsp.
- Cumin powder - 1 tsp.
- Coriander powder - 1 tsp.
- Salt - to taste.
- Pepper - to taste.
- Water - 2 cups.
- Oil - 2 tbsp.

Instructions

1. Heat oil in a pot over medium heat.

2. Sauté onions until golden brown.

3. Add garlic and ginger, and cook for 1-2 minutes.

4. Add octopus pieces and cook until browned.

5. Add chopped tomatoes and cook until soft.

6. Stir in turmeric, cumin, and coriander powders.

7. Pour in coconut milk and water, and bring to a boil.

8. Reduce heat and simmer until the octopus is tender and the sauce thickens.

9. Season with salt and pepper.

10. Serve hot with rice or chapati.

FRIED FISH

Ingredients

- Fish fillets - 1 lb.
- Garlic powder - 1 tsp.
- Onion powder - 1 tsp.
- Turmeric powder - 1/2 tsp.
- Salt - to taste.
- Pepper - to taste.
- Flour - 1 cup.
- Oil - for frying.

Instructions

1. In a bowl, mix garlic powder, onion powder, turmeric, salt, and pepper.

2. Coat the fish fillets with the spice mixture.

3. Dredge the fillets in flour, shaking off the excess.

4. Heat oil in a skillet over medium heat.

5. Fry the fish fillets until golden brown and cooked through, turning occasionally.

6. Drain on paper towels.

7. Serve hot with lemon wedges and a fresh salad.

FISH STEW

Ingredients

- Fish fillets - 1 lb, cut into pieces.
- Onion - 1, chopped.
- Garlic - 3 cloves, minced.
- Ginger - 1 tbsp, minced.
- Tomato - 2, chopped.
- Potato - 2, cubed.
- Carrot - 1, sliced.
- Fish broth - 4 cups.
- Salt - to taste.
- Pepper - to taste.
- Oil - 2 tbsp.

Instructions

1. Heat oil in a pot over medium heat.

2. Sauté onions until golden brown.

3. Add garlic and ginger, and cook for 1-2 minutes.

4. Add fish pieces and brown on all sides.

5. Add chopped tomatoes, potatoes, and carrots.

6. Pour in fish broth and bring to a boil.

7. Reduce heat and simmer until the fish and vegetables are tender.

8. Season with salt and pepper.

9. Serve hot with rice or chapati.

PRAWN CURRY

Ingredients

- Prawns - 1 lb, cleaned and deveined.
- Onion - 1, finely chopped.
- Garlic - 3 cloves, minced.
- Ginger - 1 tbsp, minced.
- Tomato - 2, chopped.
- Coconut milk - 1 cup.
- Turmeric powder - 1 tsp.
- Cumin powder - 1 tsp.
- Coriander powder - 1 tsp.
- Salt - to taste.
- Pepper - to taste.
- Water - 2 cups.
- Oil - 2 tbsp.

Instructions

1. Heat oil in a pot over medium heat.

2. Sauté onions until golden brown.

3. Add garlic and ginger, and cook for 1-2 minutes.

4. Add prawns and cook until pink.

5. Add chopped tomatoes and cook until soft.

6. Stir in turmeric, cumin, and coriander powders.

7. Pour in coconut milk and water, and bring to a boil.

8. Reduce heat and simmer until the prawns are cooked through and the sauce thickens.

9. Season with salt and pepper.

10. Serve hot with rice or chapati.

FISH AND VEGETABLE STIR FRY

Ingredients

- Fish fillets - 1 lb, cut into pieces.
- Bell pepper - 1, sliced.
- Carrot - 1, julienned.
- Onion - 1, sliced.
- Garlic - 3 cloves, minced.
- Ginger - 1 tbsp, minced.
- Soy sauce - 2 tbsp.
- Chili sauce - 1 tbsp.
- Honey - 1 tbsp.
- Salt - to taste.
- Pepper - to taste.
- Oil - 2 tbsp.

Instructions

1. Heat oil in a large skillet or wok over medium-high heat.

2. Add garlic and ginger, and cook for 1-2 minutes.

3. Add fish pieces and stir-fry until browned.

4. Add bell pepper, carrot, and onion, and stir-fry for another 3-4 minutes.

5. In a bowl, mix soy sauce, chili sauce, and honey.

6. Pour the sauce into the skillet and mix well.

7. Stir-fry until the vegetables are tender and the fish is cooked through.

8. Season with salt and pepper.

9. Serve hot with rice or noodles.

SQUID CURRY

Ingredients

- Squid - 1 lb, cleaned and cut into rings.
- Onion - 1, finely chopped.
- Garlic - 3 cloves, minced.
- Ginger - 1 tbsp, minced.
- Tomato - 2, chopped.
- Coconut milk - 1 cup.
- Turmeric powder - 1 tsp.
- Cumin powder - 1 tsp.
- Coriander powder - 1 tsp.
- Salt - to taste.
- Pepper - to taste.
- Water - 2 cups.
- Oil - 2 tbsp.

Instructions

1. Heat oil in a pot over medium heat.

2. Sauté onions until golden brown.

3. Add garlic and ginger, and cook for 1-2 minutes.

4. Add squid rings and cook until slightly browned.

5. Add chopped tomatoes and cook until soft.

6. Stir in turmeric, cumin, and coriander powders.

7. Pour in coconut milk and water, and bring to a boil.

8. Reduce heat and simmer until the squid is tender and the sauce thickens.

9. Season with salt and pepper.

10. Serve hot with rice or chapati.

FISH AND COCONUT SOUP

Ingredients

- Fish fillets - 1 lb, cut into pieces.
- Onion - 1, chopped.
- Garlic - 3 cloves, minced.
- Ginger - 1 tbsp, minced.
- Tomato - 2, chopped.
- Coconut milk - 1 cup.
- Fish broth - 4 cups.
- Turmeric powder - 1 tsp.
- Cumin powder - 1 tsp.
- Salt - to taste.
- Pepper - to taste.
- Oil - 2 tbsp.

Instructions

1. Heat oil in a pot over medium heat.

2. Sauté onions until golden brown.

3. Add garlic and ginger, and cook for 1-2 minutes.

4. Add fish pieces and cook until browned.

5. Add chopped tomatoes and cook until soft.

6. Stir in turmeric and cumin powders.

7. Pour in coconut milk and fish broth, and bring to a boil.

8. Reduce heat and simmer until the fish is cooked through.

9. Season with salt and pepper.

10. Serve hot with rice or chapati.

SEAFOOD MIXED GRILL

Ingredients

- Shrimp - 1 lb, cleaned and deveined.
- Squid - 1 lb, cleaned and cut into rings.
- Fish fillets - 1 lb, cut into pieces.
- Garlic - 3 cloves, minced.
- Ginger - 1 tbsp, minced.
- Lemon juice - 2 tbsp.
- Chili powder - 1 tsp.
- Salt - to taste.
- Pepper - to taste.
- Oil - for grilling.

Instructions

1. In a bowl, mix garlic, ginger, lemon juice, chili powder, salt, and pepper.

2. Marinate the shrimp, squid, and fish pieces in the mixture for at least 30 minutes.

3. Preheat the grill to medium-high heat and brush with oil.

4. Grill the seafood until cooked through, turning occasionally.

5. Serve hot with a side of lemon wedges and a fresh salad.

FISH KEBABS

Ingredients

- Fish fillets - 1 lb, cut into pieces.
- Bell pepper - 1, cut into chunks.
- Onion - 1, cut into chunks.
- Zucchini - 1, sliced.
- Garlic - 3 cloves, minced.
- Ginger - 1 tbsp, minced.
- Lemon juice - 2 tbsp.
- Soy sauce - 2 tbsp.
- Honey - 1 tbsp.
- Salt - to taste.
- Pepper - to taste.
- Oil - for grilling.
- Skewers - as needed.

Instructions

1. In a bowl, mix garlic, ginger, lemon juice, soy sauce, honey, salt, and pepper.

2. Add fish pieces to the marinade and coat well.

3. Marinate for at least 1 hour or overnight in the refrigerator.

4. Preheat the grill to medium-high heat and brush with oil.

5. Thread marinated fish, bell pepper, onion, and zucchini onto skewers.

6. Grill the kebabs until the fish is cooked through and the vegetables are tender, turning occasionally.

7. Serve hot with your favorite side dishes.

FISH AND BANANA CURRY

Ingredients

- Fish fillets - 1 lb, cut into pieces.
- Green bananas - 4, peeled and sliced.
- Onion - 1, chopped.
- Garlic - 3 cloves, minced.
- Ginger - 1 tbsp, minced.
- Tomato - 2, chopped.
- Coconut milk - 1 cup.
- Turmeric powder - 1 tsp.
- Cumin powder - 1 tsp.
- Coriander powder - 1 tsp.
- Salt - to taste.
- Pepper - to taste.
- Water - 2 cups.
- Oil - 2 tbsp.

Instructions

1. Heat oil in a pot over medium heat.

2. Sauté onions until golden brown.

3. Add garlic and ginger, and cook for 1-2 minutes.

4. Add fish pieces and brown on all sides.

5. Add chopped tomatoes and cook until soft.

6. Stir in turmeric, cumin, and coriander powders.

7. Add sliced bananas and mix well.

8. Pour in coconut milk and water, and bring to a boil.

9. Reduce heat and simmer until the fish and bananas are tender.

10. Season with salt and pepper.

11. Serve hot with rice or chapati.

RICE DISHES

Tanzanian rice dishes stand out due to their rich blend of flavors and significant role within the national diet, providing a staple food that is both versatile and nourishing. These dishes frequently incorporate rice cooked with coconut milk, spices like cinnamon and cardamom, and a variety of ingredients such as beans or cashews, enhancing the nutritional value and taste profile. Cooking methods such as pilau and biryani not only infuse the rice with aromatic spices but also lock in nutrients, making each serving both flavorful and healthful.

The adaptability of rice in Tanzanian cuisine is showcased in its ability to merge with different components, creating meals that are adaptable to various dietary needs and preferences. From simple white rice served with fish to complex spiced rice dishes cooked with meat or vegetables, each preparation reflects a piece of Tanzania's diverse culinary landscape. This versatility ensures that rice is a fundamental component of both everyday eating and festive occasions.

Rice dishes in Tanzania are celebrated not only for their satisfying flavors but also for their role in a balanced diet. They are a crucial source of energy, providing carbohydrates that are essential for day-to-day activities.

PILAU

Ingredients

- Basmati rice - 2 cups.
- Beef or chicken - 1 lb, cubed.
- Onion - 1, chopped.

- Garlic - 3 cloves, minced.
- Ginger - 1 tbsp, minced.
- Tomato - 2, chopped.
- Potato - 2, cubed.
- Carrot - 1, chopped.
- Cumin seeds - 1 tsp.
- Cardamom pods - 4.
- Cinnamon stick - 1.
- Cloves - 4.
- Salt - to taste.
- Water - 4 cups.
- Oil - 3 tbsp.

Instructions

1. Heat oil in a large pot over medium heat.

2. Sauté onions until golden brown.

3. Add garlic, ginger, and whole spices (cumin, cardamom, cinnamon, cloves) and cook for 1-2 minutes.

4. Add meat and brown on all sides.

5. Stir in chopped tomatoes, potatoes, and carrots.

6. Add rice and mix well.

7. Pour in water and bring to a boil.

8. Reduce heat, cover, and simmer until the rice is cooked and the liquid is absorbed.

9. Season with salt.

10. Serve hot.

WALI WA NAZI (COCONUT RICE)

Ingredients

- Basmati rice - 2 cups.
- Coconut milk - 2 cups.
- Water - 2 cups.
- Salt - to taste.
- Oil - 1 tbsp.

Instructions

1. Rinse the rice under cold water until the water runs clear.

2. Heat oil in a large pot over medium heat.

3. Add the rice and stir to coat with the oil.

4. Pour in coconut milk, water, and salt.

5. Bring to a boil, then reduce heat to low.

6. Cover and simmer until the rice is cooked and the liquid is absorbed.

7. Fluff the rice with a fork and serve hot.

BIRYANI

Ingredients

- Basmati rice - 2 cups.
- Chicken or beef - 1 lb, cubed.
- Onion - 1, finely chopped.
- Garlic - 3 cloves, minced.
- Ginger - 1 tbsp, minced.

- Tomato - 2, chopped.
- Yogurt - 1 cup.
- Mint leaves - 1/4 cup, chopped.
- Cilantro - 1/4 cup, chopped.
- Cumin powder - 1 tsp.
- Coriander powder - 1 tsp.
- Turmeric powder - 1/2 tsp.
- Salt - to taste.
- Water - 4 cups.
- Oil - 3 tbsp.

Instructions

1. Heat oil in a large pot over medium heat.

2. Sauté onions until golden brown.

3. Add garlic, ginger, cumin, coriander, and turmeric powders and cook for 1-2 minutes.

4. Add meat and brown on all sides.

5. Stir in chopped tomatoes and yogurt.

6. Add mint leaves and cilantro.

7. Add rice and mix well.

8. Pour in water and bring to a boil.

9. Reduce heat, cover, and simmer until the rice is cooked and the liquid is absorbed.

10. Season with salt.

11. Serve hot.

WALI WA KUKAANGA (FRIED RICE)

Ingredients

- Cooked rice - 4 cups.
- Eggs - 2, beaten.
- Onion - 1, chopped.
- Garlic - 3 cloves, minced.
- Carrot - 1, chopped.
- Peas - 1 cup.
- Soy sauce - 3 tbsp.
- Salt - to taste.
- Pepper - to taste.
- Oil - 3 tbsp.

Instructions

1. Heat oil in a large skillet or wok over medium heat.

2. Add beaten eggs and scramble until cooked. Remove and set aside.

3. In the same skillet, add more oil if needed and sauté onions until golden brown.

4. Add garlic and cook for 1-2 minutes.

5. Add chopped carrots and peas, and cook until tender.

6. Stir in cooked rice and scrambled eggs.

7. Add soy sauce, salt, and pepper, and mix well.

8. Cook for another 2-3 minutes, stirring frequently.

9. Serve hot.

WALI NA SAMAKI (RICE WITH FISH)

Ingredients

- Basmati rice - 2 cups.
- Fish fillets - 1 lb, cut into pieces.
- Onion - 1, chopped.
- Garlic - 3 cloves, minced.
- Ginger - 1 tbsp, minced.
- Tomato - 2, chopped.
- Coconut milk - 1 cup.
- Water - 2 cups.
- Turmeric powder - 1 tsp.
- Cumin powder - 1 tsp.
- Coriander powder - 1 tsp.
- Salt - to taste.
- Pepper - to taste.
- Oil - 3 tbsp.

Instructions

1. Heat oil in a large pot over medium heat.

2. Sauté onions until golden brown.

3. Add garlic and ginger, and cook for 1-2 minutes.

4. Add fish pieces and cook until browned.

5. Add chopped tomatoes and cook until soft.

6. Stir in turmeric, cumin, and coriander powders.

7. Add rice and mix well.

8. Pour in coconut milk and water, and bring to a boil.

9. Reduce heat, cover, and simmer until the rice is cooked and the liquid is absorbed.

10. Season with salt and pepper.

11. Serve hot.

WALI NA MAHARAGE (RICE WITH BEANS)

Ingredients

- Basmati rice - 2 cups.
- Cooked beans - 2 cups.
- Onion - 1, chopped.
- Garlic - 3 cloves, minced.
- Tomato - 2, chopped.
- Coconut milk - 1 cup.
- Water - 2 cups.
- Salt - to taste.
- Pepper - to taste.
- Oil - 2 tbsp.

Instructions

1. Heat oil in a large pot over medium heat.

2. Sauté onions until golden brown.

3. Add garlic and cook for 1-2 minutes.

4. Add chopped tomatoes and cook until soft.

5. Add cooked beans and stir well.

6. Add rice and mix well.

7. Pour in coconut milk and water, and bring to a boil.

8. Reduce heat, cover, and simmer until the rice is cooked and the liquid is absorbed.

9. Season with salt and pepper.

10. Serve hot.

WALI WA KAROTI (CARROT RICE)

Ingredients

- Basmati rice - 2 cups.
- Carrot - 2, grated.
- Onion - 1, chopped.
- Garlic - 3 cloves, minced.
- Ginger - 1 tbsp, minced.
- Cumin seeds - 1 tsp.
- Cinnamon stick - 1.
- Cardamom pods - 4.
- Cloves - 4.
- Salt - to taste.
- Water - 4 cups.
- Oil - 2 tbsp.

Instructions

1. Heat oil in a large pot over medium heat.

2. Sauté onions until golden brown.

3. Add garlic and ginger, and cook for 1-2 minutes.

4. Add cumin seeds, cinnamon, cardamom, and cloves, and cook for 1-2 minutes.

5. Add grated carrots and stir well.

6. Add rice and mix well.

7. Pour in water and bring to a boil.

8. Reduce heat, cover, and simmer until the rice is cooked and the liquid is absorbed.

9. Season with salt. Serve hot.

WALI WA ZAFARANI (SAFFRON RICE)

Ingredients

- Basmati rice - 2 cups.
- Saffron threads - 1/4 tsp.
- Onion - 1, chopped.
- Garlic - 3 cloves, minced.
- Ginger - 1 tbsp, minced.
- Cumin seeds - 1 tsp.
- Cinnamon stick - 1.
- Cardamom pods - 4.
- Cloves - 4.
- Salt - to taste.
- Water - 4 cups.
- Oil - 2 tbsp.

Instructions

1. Soak saffron threads in a small amount of warm water and set aside.

2. Heat oil in a large pot over medium heat.

3. Sauté onions until golden brown.

4. Add garlic and ginger, and cook for 1-2 minutes.

5. Add cumin seeds, cinnamon, cardamom, and cloves, and cook for 1-2 minutes.

6. Add rice and mix well.

7. Pour in water and saffron mixture, and bring to a boil.

8. Reduce heat, cover, and simmer until the rice is cooked and the liquid is absorbed.

9. Season with salt. Serve hot.

WALI WA TENDE (DATE RICE)

Ingredients

- Basmati rice - 2 cups.
- Dates - 1 cup, pitted and chopped.
- Onion - 1, chopped.
- Garlic - 3 cloves, minced.
- Ginger - 1 tbsp, minced.
- Cumin seeds - 1 tsp.
- Cinnamon stick - 1.
- Cardamom pods - 4.
- Cloves - 4.
- Salt - to taste.
- Water - 4 cups.
- Oil - 2 tbsp.

Instructions

1. Heat oil in a large pot over medium heat.

2. Sauté onions until golden brown.

3. Add garlic and ginger, and cook for 1-2 minutes.

4. Add cumin seeds, cinnamon, cardamom, and cloves, and cook for 1-2 minutes.

5. Add chopped dates and stir well.

6. Add rice and mix well.

7. Pour in water and bring to a boil.

8. Reduce heat, cover, and simmer until the rice is cooked and the liquid is absorbed.

9. Season with salt.

10. Serve hot.

WALI WA KUNDE (COWPEA RICE)

Ingredients

- Basmati rice - 2 cups.
- Cooked cowpeas - 2 cups.
- Onion - 1, chopped.
- Garlic - 3 cloves, minced.
- Tomato - 2, chopped.
- Coconut milk - 1 cup.
- Water - 2 cups.
- Salt - to taste.
- Pepper - to taste.
- Oil - 2 tbsp.

Instructions

1. Heat oil in a large pot over medium heat.

2. Sauté onions until golden brown.

3. Add garlic and cook for 1-2 minutes.

4. Add chopped tomatoes and cook until soft.

5. Add cooked cowpeas and stir well.

6. Add rice and mix well.

7. Pour in coconut milk and water, and bring to a boil.

8. Reduce heat, cover, and simmer until the rice is cooked and the liquid is absorbed.

9. Season with salt and pepper.

10. Serve hot.

BEANS

Beans in Tanzanian cuisine are integral, celebrated for their versatility and nutritional benefits, distinguishing them from other staple ingredients. These legumes are incorporated into various dishes, often paired with grains like rice or maize, enhancing both their flavor and protein content. The preparation methods, ranging from boiling to stewing with spices and vegetables, not only enrich the dishes' flavors but also their overall nutritional profile.

The adaptability of beans is evident in their presence across a spectrum of Tanzanian dishes, from simple bean soups to more complex stews that include meat and vegetables. This flexibility allows beans to be a dietary mainstay, suitable for vegetarians and meat-eaters alike. By absorbing the flavors of accompanying spices and ingredients, beans serve as a hearty base in both everyday meals and celebratory feasts.

Bean dishes in Tanzania are valued not just for their flavor but also for their role in promoting health. Rich in fiber and protein, they contribute to a balanced diet, supporting overall well-being.

MAHARAGE YA NAZI
(BEANS IN COCONUT SAUCE)

Ingredients

- Red kidney beans - 2 cups, cooked.
- Onion - 1, chopped.
- Garlic - 3 cloves, minced.
- Ginger - 1 tbsp, minced.
- Tomato - 2, chopped.
- Coconut milk - 1 cup.

- Water - 1 cup.
- Turmeric powder - 1 tsp.
- Salt - to taste.
- Pepper - to taste.
- Oil - 2 tbsp.

Instructions

1. Heat oil in a pot over medium heat.

2. Sauté onions until golden brown.

3. Add garlic and ginger, and cook for 1-2 minutes.

4. Add chopped tomatoes and cook until soft.

5. Add cooked beans and stir well.

6. Pour in coconut milk, water, and turmeric powder.

7. Bring to a boil, then reduce heat and simmer for 15-20 minutes.

8. Season with salt and pepper.

9. Serve hot with rice or chapati.

MAHARAGE
(RED KIDNEY BEANS STEW)

Ingredients

- Red kidney beans - 2 cups, cooked.
- Onion - 1, chopped.
- Garlic - 3 cloves, minced.
- Ginger - 1 tbsp, minced.
- Tomato - 2, chopped.

- Carrot - 1, chopped.
- Tomato paste - 2 tbsp.
- Water - 2 cups.
- Salt - to taste.
- Pepper - to taste.
- Oil - 2 tbsp.

Instructions

1. Heat oil in a pot over medium heat.

2. Sauté onions until golden brown.

3. Add garlic and ginger, and cook for 1-2 minutes.

4. Add chopped tomatoes, carrots, and tomato paste.

5. Cook until the tomatoes are soft.

6. Add cooked beans and stir well.

7. Pour in water and bring to a boil.

8. Reduce heat and simmer for 15-20 minutes.

9. Season with salt and pepper.

10. Serve hot with rice or chapati.

FRIED BEANS

Ingredients

- Beans (any type) - 2 cups, cooked.
- Onion - 1, chopped.
- Garlic - 3 cloves, minced.
- Tomato - 2, chopped.

- Green bell pepper - 1, chopped.
- Salt - to taste.
- Pepper - to taste.
- Oil - 2 tbsp.

Instructions

1. Heat oil in a skillet over medium heat.

2. Sauté onions until golden brown.

3. Add garlic and cook for 1-2 minutes.

4. Add chopped tomatoes and green bell pepper, and cook until soft.

5. Add cooked beans and stir well.

6. Cook for another 5-10 minutes, stirring occasionally.

7. Season with salt and pepper.

8. Serve hot with rice or chapati.

BEAN SOUP

Ingredients

- Beans (any type) - 2 cups, cooked.
- Onion - 1, chopped.
- Garlic - 3 cloves, minced.
- Ginger - 1 tbsp, minced.
- Tomato - 2, chopped.
- Carrot - 1, chopped.
- Celery - 1 stalk, chopped.
- Vegetable broth - 4 cups.
- Salt - to taste.

- Pepper - to taste.
- Oil - 2 tbsp.

Instructions

1. Heat oil in a pot over medium heat.

2. Sauté onions until golden brown.

3. Add garlic and ginger, and cook for 1-2 minutes.

4. Add chopped tomatoes, carrots, and celery.

5. Cook until the vegetables are tender.

6. Add cooked beans and vegetable broth.

7. Bring to a boil, then reduce heat and simmer for 15-20 minutes.

8. Season with salt and pepper.

9. Serve hot.

BEAN STEW

Ingredients

- Beans (any type) - 2 cups, cooked.
- Onion - 1, chopped.
- Garlic - 3 cloves, minced.
- Ginger - 1 tbsp, minced.
- Tomato - 2, chopped.
- Potato - 2, cubed.
- Carrot - 1, chopped.
- Tomato paste - 2 tbsp.
- Water - 2 cups.

- Salt - to taste.
- Pepper - to taste.
- Oil - 2 tbsp.

Instructions

1. Heat oil in a pot over medium heat.

2. Sauté onions until golden brown.

3. Add garlic and ginger, and cook for 1-2 minutes.

4. Add chopped tomatoes, potatoes, carrots, and tomato paste.

5. Cook until the tomatoes are soft.

6. Add cooked beans and stir well.

7. Pour in water and bring to a boil.

8. Reduce heat and simmer for 15-20 minutes.

9. Season with salt and pepper.

10. Serve hot with rice or chapati.

BEANS AND VEGETABLES

Ingredients

- Beans (any type) - 2 cups, cooked.
- Onion - 1, chopped.
- Garlic - 3 cloves, minced.
- Carrot - 1, chopped.
- Bell pepper - 1, chopped.
- Tomato - 2, chopped.

- Salt - to taste.
- Pepper - to taste.
- Oil - 2 tbsp.

Instructions

1. Heat oil in a skillet over medium heat.

2. Sauté onions until golden brown.

3. Add garlic and cook for 1-2 minutes.

4. Add chopped carrots and bell pepper, and cook until tender.

5. Add chopped tomatoes and cook until soft.

6. Add cooked beans and stir well.

7. Season with salt and pepper.

8. Cook for another 5-10 minutes, stirring occasionally.

9. Serve hot with rice or chapati.

BEAN CURRY

Ingredients

- Beans (any type) - 2 cups, cooked.
- Onion - 1, chopped.
- Garlic - 3 cloves, minced.
- Ginger - 1 tbsp, minced.
- Tomato - 2, chopped.
- Coconut milk - 1 cup.
- Water - 1 cup.
- Turmeric powder - 1 tsp.

- Cumin powder - 1 tsp.
- Coriander powder - 1 tsp.
- Salt - to taste.
- Pepper - to taste.
- Oil - 2 tbsp.

Instructions

1. Heat oil in a pot over medium heat.
2. Sauté onions until golden brown.
3. Add garlic and ginger, and cook for 1-2 minutes.
4. Add chopped tomatoes and cook until soft.
5. Stir in turmeric, cumin, and coriander powders.
6. Add cooked beans and mix well.
7. Pour in coconut milk and water, and bring to a boil.
8. Reduce heat and simmer for 15-20 minutes.
9. Season with salt and pepper.
10. Serve hot with rice or chapati.

BEANS WITH SPINACH

Ingredients

- Beans (any type) - 2 cups, cooked.
- Spinach - 1 bunch, chopped.
- Onion - 1, chopped.
- Garlic - 3 cloves, minced.
- Tomato - 2, chopped.

- Salt - to taste.
- Pepper - to taste.
- Oil - 2 tbsp.

Instructions

1. Heat oil in a skillet over medium heat.

2. Sauté onions until golden brown.

3. Add garlic and cook for 1-2 minutes.

4. Add chopped tomatoes and cook until soft.

5. Add chopped spinach and cook until wilted.

6. Add cooked beans and stir well.

7. Season with salt and pepper.

8. Cook for another 5-10 minutes, stirring occasionally.

9. Serve hot with rice or chapati.

BEANS AND RICE

Ingredients

- Basmati rice - 2 cups.
- Beans (any type) - 2 cups, cooked.
- Onion - 1, chopped.
- Garlic - 3 cloves, minced.
- Tomato - 2, chopped.
- Coconut milk - 1 cup.
- Water - 2 cups.
- Salt - to taste.
- Pepper - to taste.

- Oil - 2 tbsp.

Instructions

1. Heat oil in a large pot over medium heat.

2. Sauté onions until golden brown.

3. Add garlic and cook for 1-2 minutes.

4. Add chopped tomatoes and cook until soft.

5. Add cooked beans and stir well.

6. Add rice and mix well.

7. Pour in coconut milk and water, and bring to a boil.

8. Reduce heat, cover, and simmer until the rice is cooked and the liquid is absorbed.

9. Season with salt and pepper.

10. Serve hot.

BEANS AND BANANA STEW

Ingredients

- Beans (any type) - 2 cups, cooked.
- Green bananas - 4, peeled and sliced.
- Onion - 1, chopped.
- Garlic - 3 cloves, minced.
- Ginger - 1 tbsp, minced.
- Tomato - 2, chopped.
- Coconut milk - 1 cup.
- Water - 2 cups.

- Turmeric powder - 1 tsp.
- Salt - to taste.
- Pepper - to taste.
- Oil - 2 tbsp.

Instructions

1. Heat oil in a pot over medium heat.

2. Sauté onions until golden brown.

3. Add garlic and ginger, and cook for 1-2 minutes.

4. Add chopped tomatoes and cook until soft.

5. Stir in turmeric powder.

6. Add cooked beans and sliced bananas, and mix well.

7. Pour in coconut milk and water, and bring to a boil.

8. Reduce heat and simmer for 15-20 minutes.

9. Season with salt and pepper.

10. Serve hot with rice or chapati.

SWEET BEANS

Ingredients

- Red kidney beans - 2 cups, cooked.
- Onion - 1, chopped.
- Garlic - 3 cloves, minced.
- Ginger - 1 tbsp, minced.
- Tomato - 2, chopped.
- Coconut milk - 1 cup.

- Brown sugar - 2 tbsp.
- Salt - to taste.
- Pepper - to taste.
- Oil - 2 tbsp.

Instructions

1. Heat oil in a pot over medium heat.

2. Sauté onions until golden brown.

3. Add garlic and ginger, and cook for 1-2 minutes.

4. Add chopped tomatoes and cook until soft.

5. Add cooked beans and stir well.

6. Pour in coconut milk and brown sugar.

7. Bring to a boil, then reduce heat and simmer for 15-20 minutes.

8. Season with salt and pepper.

9. Serve hot with rice or chapati.

SPICY BEANS

Ingredients

- Beans (any type) - 2 cups, cooked.
- Onion - 1, chopped.
- Garlic - 3 cloves, minced.
- Ginger - 1 tbsp, minced.
- Tomato - 2, chopped.
- Green chili - 2, chopped.
- Cumin powder - 1 tsp.

- Turmeric powder - 1 tsp.
- Salt - to taste.
- Pepper - to taste.
- Oil - 2 tbsp.

Instructions

1. Heat oil in a pot over medium heat.

2. Sauté onions until golden brown.

3. Add garlic, ginger, and green chili, and cook for 1-2 minutes.

4. Add chopped tomatoes and cook until soft.

5. Stir in cumin and turmeric powders.

6. Add cooked beans and mix well.

7. Cook for another 5-10 minutes, stirring occasionally.

8. Season with salt and pepper.

9. Serve hot with rice or chapati.

BEANS AND CORN

Ingredients

- Beans (any type) - 2 cups, cooked.
- Fresh corn kernels - 1 cup.
- Onion - 1, chopped.
- Garlic - 3 cloves, minced.
- Tomato - 2, chopped.
- Salt - to taste.
- Pepper - to taste.

- Oil - 2 tbsp.

Instructions

1. Heat oil in a skillet over medium heat.

2. Sauté onions until golden brown.

3. Add garlic and cook for 1-2 minutes.

4. Add chopped tomatoes and cook until soft.

5. Add fresh corn kernels and cook for 5-7 minutes.

6. Add cooked beans and stir well.

7. Season with salt and pepper.

8. Cook for another 5-10 minutes, stirring occasionally.

9. Serve hot with rice or chapati.

BEANS AND POTATO STEW

Ingredients

- Beans (any type) - 2 cups, cooked.
- Potato - 2, cubed.
- Onion - 1, chopped.
- Garlic - 3 cloves, minced.
- Ginger - 1 tbsp, minced.
- Tomato - 2, chopped.
- Tomato paste - 2 tbsp.
- Water - 2 cups.
- Salt - to taste.
- Pepper - to taste.
- Oil - 2 tbsp.

Instructions

1. Heat oil in a pot over medium heat.

2. Sauté onions until golden brown.

3. Add garlic and ginger, and cook for 1-2 minutes.

4. Add chopped tomatoes and tomato paste, and cook until soft.

5. Add cubed potatoes and stir well.

6. Pour in water and bring to a boil.

7. Reduce heat and simmer until the potatoes are tender.

8. Add cooked beans and mix well.

9. Season with salt and pepper.

10. Serve hot with rice or chapati.

BEANS AND TOMATO SAUCE

Ingredients

- Beans (any type) - 2 cups, cooked.
- Onion - 1, chopped.
- Garlic - 3 cloves, minced.
- Tomato - 2, chopped.
- Tomato sauce - 1 cup.
- Salt - to taste.
- Pepper - to taste.
- Oil - 2 tbsp.

Instructions

1. Heat oil in a skillet over medium heat.

2. Sauté onions until golden brown.

3. Add garlic and cook for 1-2 minutes.

4. Add chopped tomatoes and cook until soft.

5. Add tomato sauce and stir well.

6. Add cooked beans and mix well.

7. Season with salt and pepper.

8. Cook for another 5-10 minutes, stirring occasionally.

9. Serve hot with rice or chapati.

LEGUMES

Legumes play a crucial role in Tanzanian cuisine, standing out for their versatility and rich nutritional value, distinguishing them from other staple foods. They are incorporated in a variety of dishes, ranging from soups and stews to salads, where they provide essential proteins and fibers. The preparation of legumes often involves simmering with aromatic herbs and spices, which not only enhances their flavor but also maximizes their health benefits.

The adaptability of legumes in Tanzanian dishes is seen in their ability to blend with a multitude of ingredients, creating satisfying meals that cater to diverse dietary preferences. Whether cooked with meats in hearty stews or combined with grains in pilafs, legumes absorb flavors well and add substantial texture to dishes. This makes them a favored ingredient among those who value both taste and nutritional content.

Legumes are a dietary cornerstone in Tanzania, appreciated not just for their culinary flexibility but also for their contribution to a healthy diet. They are a fundamental part of the Tanzanian diet, promoting better health through their high nutrient content.

DENGU (LENTIL CURRY)

Ingredients

- Red lentils - 1 cup.
- Onion - 1, chopped.
- Garlic - 3 cloves, minced.
- Ginger - 1 tbsp, minced.
- Tomato - 2, chopped.

- Coconut milk - 1 cup.
- Water - 2 cups.
- Turmeric powder - 1 tsp.
- Cumin powder - 1 tsp.
- Coriander powder - 1 tsp.
- Salt - to taste.
- Pepper - to taste.
- Oil - 2 tbsp.

Instructions

1. Heat oil in a pot over medium heat.

2. Sauté onions until golden brown.

3. Add garlic and ginger, and cook for 1-2 minutes.

4. Add chopped tomatoes and cook until soft.

5. Stir in turmeric, cumin, and coriander powders.

6. Add lentils and mix well.

7. Pour in coconut milk and water, and bring to a boil.

8. Reduce heat and simmer until the lentils are tender and the sauce thickens.

9. Season with salt and pepper.

10. Serve hot with rice or chapati.

CHICKPEA CURRY

Ingredients

- Chickpeas - 2 cups, cooked.

- Onion - 1, chopped.
- Garlic - 3 cloves, minced.
- Ginger - 1 tbsp, minced.
- Tomato - 2, chopped.
- Coconut milk - 1 cup.
- Water - 1 cup.
- Turmeric powder - 1 tsp.
- Cumin powder - 1 tsp.
- Coriander powder - 1 tsp.
- Salt - to taste.
- Pepper - to taste.
- Oil - 2 tbsp.

Instructions

1. Heat oil in a pot over medium heat.
2. Sauté onions until golden brown.
3. Add garlic and ginger, and cook for 1-2 minutes.
4. Add chopped tomatoes and cook until soft.
5. Stir in turmeric, cumin, and coriander powders.
6. Add cooked chickpeas and mix well.
7. Pour in coconut milk and water, and bring to a boil.
8. Reduce heat and simmer for 15-20 minutes.
9. Season with salt and pepper.
10. Serve hot with rice or chapati.

PIGEON PEA STEW

Ingredients

- Pigeon peas - 2 cups, cooked.
- Onion - 1, chopped.
- Garlic - 3 cloves, minced.
- Ginger - 1 tbsp, minced.
- Tomato - 2, chopped.
- Coconut milk - 1 cup.
- Water - 2 cups.
- Turmeric powder - 1 tsp.
- Cumin powder - 1 tsp.
- Coriander powder - 1 tsp.
- Salt - to taste.
- Pepper - to taste.
- Oil - 2 tbsp.

Instructions

1. Heat oil in a pot over medium heat.
2. Sauté onions until golden brown.
3. Add garlic and ginger, and cook for 1-2 minutes.
4. Add chopped tomatoes and cook until soft.
5. Stir in turmeric, cumin, and coriander powders.
6. Add cooked pigeon peas and mix well.
7. Pour in coconut milk and water, and bring to a boil.
8. Reduce heat and simmer for 15-20 minutes.
9. Season with salt and pepper.

10. Serve hot with rice or chapati.

LENTIL SOUP

Ingredients

- Red lentils - 1 cup.
- Onion - 1, chopped.
- Garlic - 3 cloves, minced.
- Ginger - 1 tbsp, minced.
- Carrot - 1, chopped.
- Celery - 1 stalk, chopped.
- Tomato - 2, chopped.
- Vegetable broth - 4 cups.
- Turmeric powder - 1 tsp.
- Cumin powder - 1 tsp.
- Salt - to taste.
- Pepper - to taste.
- Oil - 2 tbsp.

Instructions

1. Heat oil in a pot over medium heat.

2. Sauté onions until golden brown.

3. Add garlic and ginger, and cook for 1-2 minutes.

4. Add chopped carrots, celery, and tomatoes, and cook until soft.

5. Stir in turmeric and cumin powders.

6. Add lentils and mix well.

7. Pour in vegetable broth and bring to a boil.

8. Reduce heat and simmer until the lentils are tender.

9. Season with salt and pepper.

10. Serve hot with bread.

CHICKPEA SALAD

Ingredients

- Chickpeas - 2 cups, cooked.
- Cucumber - 1, diced.
- Tomato - 2, chopped.
- Red onion - 1, finely chopped.
- Parsley - 1/4 cup, chopped.
- Lemon juice - 2 tbsp.
- Olive oil - 2 tbsp.
- Salt - to taste.
- Pepper - to taste.

Instructions

1. In a large bowl, combine cooked chickpeas, diced cucumber, chopped tomatoes, and finely chopped red onion.

2. Add chopped parsley and mix well.

3. In a small bowl, whisk together lemon juice, olive oil, salt, and pepper.

4. Pour the dressing over the salad and toss to coat.

5. Serve chilled.

LENTIL AND VEGETABLE STIR FRY

Ingredients

- Red lentils - 1 cup, cooked.
- Bell pepper - 1, sliced.
- Carrot - 1, julienned.
- Onion - 1, sliced.
- Garlic - 3 cloves, minced.
- Ginger - 1 tbsp, minced.
- Soy sauce - 2 tbsp.
- Chili sauce - 1 tbsp.
- Honey - 1 tbsp.
- Salt - to taste.
- Pepper - to taste.
- Oil - 2 tbsp.

Instructions

1. Heat oil in a large skillet or wok over medium-high heat.

2. Add garlic and ginger, and cook for 1-2 minutes.

3. Add bell pepper, carrot, and onion, and stir-fry for 3-4 minutes.

4. Add cooked lentils and mix well.

5. In a bowl, mix soy sauce, chili sauce, and honey.

6. Pour the sauce into the skillet and mix well.

7. Stir-fry until the vegetables are tender and the lentils are heated through.

8. Season with salt and pepper.

9. Serve hot with rice or noodles.

PIGEON PEAS AND RICE

Ingredients

- Basmati rice - 2 cups.
- Pigeon peas - 2 cups, cooked.
- Onion - 1, chopped.
- Garlic - 3 cloves, minced.
- Ginger - 1 tbsp, minced.
- Tomato - 2, chopped.
- Coconut milk - 1 cup.
- Water - 2 cups.
- Turmeric powder - 1 tsp.
- Salt - to taste.
- Pepper - to taste.
- Oil - 2 tbsp.

Instructions

1. Heat oil in a large pot over medium heat.

2. Sauté onions until golden brown.

3. Add garlic and ginger, and cook for 1-2 minutes.

4. Add chopped tomatoes and cook until soft.

5. Add cooked pigeon peas and stir well.

6. Add rice and mix well.

7. Pour in coconut milk, water, and turmeric powder, and bring to a boil.

8. Reduce heat, cover, and simmer until the rice is cooked

and the liquid is absorbed.

9. Season with salt and pepper.

10. Serve hot.

LENTIL PILAU

Ingredients

- Basmati rice - 2 cups.
- Red lentils - 1 cup, cooked.
- Onion - 1, chopped.
- Garlic - 3 cloves, minced.
- Ginger - 1 tbsp, minced.
- Tomato - 2, chopped.
- Cumin seeds - 1 tsp.
- Cardamom pods - 4.
- Cinnamon stick - 1.
- Cloves - 4.
- Salt - to taste.
- Water - 4 cups.
- Oil - 3 tbsp.

Instructions

1. Heat oil in a large pot over medium heat.

2. Sauté onions until golden brown.

3. Add garlic, ginger, cumin seeds, cardamom, cinnamon, and cloves, and cook for 1-2 minutes.

4. Add chopped tomatoes and cook until soft.

5. Add cooked lentils and stir well.

6. Add rice and mix well.

7. Pour in water and bring to a boil.

8. Reduce heat, cover, and simmer until the rice is cooked and the liquid is absorbed.

9. Season with salt.

10. Serve hot.

CHICKPEA STEW

Ingredients

- Chickpeas - 2 cups, cooked.
- Onion - 1, chopped.
- Garlic - 3 cloves, minced.
- Ginger - 1 tbsp, minced.
- Tomato - 2, chopped.
- Potato - 2, cubed.
- Carrot - 1, chopped.
- Tomato paste - 2 tbsp.
- Water - 2 cups.
- Salt - to taste.
- Pepper - to taste.
- Oil - 2 tbsp.

Instructions

1. Heat oil in a pot over medium heat.

2. Sauté onions until golden brown.

3. Add garlic and ginger, and cook for 1-2 minutes.

4. Add chopped tomatoes and tomato paste, and cook

until soft.

5. Add cubed potatoes and chopped carrots, and stir well.

6. Pour in water and bring to a boil.

7. Reduce heat and simmer until the potatoes and carrots are tender.

8. Add cooked chickpeas and mix well.

9. Season with salt and pepper.

10. Serve hot with rice or chapati.

PIGEON PEA SOUP

Ingredients

- Pigeon peas - 2 cups, cooked.
- Onion - 1, chopped.
- Garlic - 3 cloves, minced.
- Ginger - 1 tbsp, minced.
- Tomato - 2, chopped.
- Carrot - 1, chopped.
- Celery - 1 stalk, chopped.
- Vegetable broth - 4 cups.
- Turmeric powder - 1 tsp.
- Cumin powder - 1 tsp.
- Salt - to taste.
- Pepper - to taste.
- Oil - 2 tbsp.

Instructions

1. Heat oil in a pot over medium heat.

2. Sauté onions until golden brown.

3. Add garlic and ginger, and cook for 1-2 minutes.

4. Add chopped carrots, celery, and tomatoes, and cook until soft.

5. Stir in turmeric and cumin powders.

6. Add cooked pigeon peas and mix well.

7. Pour in vegetable broth and bring to a boil.

8. Reduce heat and simmer until the vegetables are tender.

9. Season with salt and pepper.

10. Serve hot with bread.

LENTIL AND BANANA STEW

Ingredients

- Red lentils - 1 cup.
- Green bananas - 4, peeled and sliced.
- Onion - 1, chopped.
- Garlic - 3 cloves, minced.
- Ginger - 1 tbsp, minced.
- Tomato - 2, chopped.
- Coconut milk - 1 cup.
- Water - 2 cups.
- Turmeric powder - 1 tsp.
- Salt - to taste.
- Pepper - to taste.
- Oil - 2 tbsp.

Instructions

1. Heat oil in a pot over medium heat.

2. Sauté onions until golden brown.

3. Add garlic and ginger, and cook for 1-2 minutes.

4. Add chopped tomatoes and cook until soft.

5. Stir in turmeric powder.

6. Add lentils and sliced bananas, and mix well.

7. Pour in coconut milk and water, and bring to a boil.

8. Reduce heat and simmer until the lentils and bananas are tender.

9. Season with salt and pepper.

10. Serve hot with rice or chapati.

CHICKPEA AND SPINACH STEW

Ingredients

- Chickpeas - 2 cups, cooked.
- Spinach - 1 bunch, chopped.
- Onion - 1, chopped.
- Garlic - 3 cloves, minced.
- Ginger - 1 tbsp, minced.
- Tomato - 2, chopped.
- Coconut milk - 1 cup.
- Water - 1 cup.
- Turmeric powder - 1 tsp.
- Salt - to taste.

- Pepper - to taste.
- Oil - 2 tbsp.

Instructions

1. Heat oil in a pot over medium heat.

2. Sauté onions until golden brown.

3. Add garlic and ginger, and cook for 1-2 minutes.

4. Add chopped tomatoes and cook until soft.

5. Stir in turmeric powder.

6. Add cooked chickpeas and mix well.

7. Pour in coconut milk and water, and bring to a boil.

8. Reduce heat and simmer for 15-20 minutes.

9. Add chopped spinach and cook until wilted.

10. Season with salt and pepper.

11. Serve hot with rice or chapati.

LENTILS WITH COCONUT

Ingredients

- Red lentils - 1 cup.
- Onion - 1, chopped.
- Garlic - 3 cloves, minced.
- Ginger - 1 tbsp, minced.
- Tomato - 2, chopped.
- Coconut milk - 1 cup.

- Water - 2 cups.
- Turmeric powder - 1 tsp.
- Salt - to taste.
- Pepper - to taste.
- Oil - 2 tbsp.

Instructions

1. Heat oil in a pot over medium heat.

2. Sauté onions until golden brown.

3. Add garlic and ginger, and cook for 1-2 minutes.

4. Add chopped tomatoes and cook until soft.

5. Stir in turmeric powder.

6. Add lentils and mix well.

7. Pour in coconut milk and water, and bring to a boil.

8. Reduce heat and simmer until the lentils are tender and the sauce thickens.

9. Season with salt and pepper.

10. Serve hot with rice or chapati.

PIGEON PEAS AND BANANA CURRY

Ingredients

- Pigeon peas - 2 cups, cooked.
- Green bananas - 4, peeled and sliced.
- Onion - 1, chopped.
- Garlic - 3 cloves, minced.

- Ginger - 1 tbsp, minced.
- Tomato - 2, chopped.
- Coconut milk - 1 cup.
- Water - 2 cups.
- Turmeric powder - 1 tsp.
- Salt - to taste.
- Pepper - to taste.
- Oil - 2 tbsp.

Instructions

1. Heat oil in a pot over medium heat.

2. Sauté onions until golden brown.

3. Add garlic and ginger, and cook for 1-2 minutes.

4. Add chopped tomatoes and cook until soft.

5. Stir in turmeric powder.

6. Add cooked pigeon peas and sliced bananas, and mix well.

7. Pour in coconut milk and water, and bring to a boil.

8. Reduce heat and simmer until the bananas are tender and the sauce thickens.

9. Season with salt and pepper.

10. Serve hot with rice or chapati.

CHICKPEA AND POTATO CURRY

Ingredients

- Chickpeas - 2 cups, cooked.
- Potato - 2, cubed.
- Onion - 1, chopped.
- Garlic - 3 cloves, minced.
- Ginger - 1 tbsp, minced.
- Tomato - 2, chopped.
- Coconut milk - 1 cup.
- Water - 2 cups.
- Turmeric powder - 1 tsp.
- Cumin powder - 1 tsp.
- Coriander powder - 1 tsp.
- Salt - to taste.
- Pepper - to taste.
- Oil - 2 tbsp.

Instructions

1. Heat oil in a pot over medium heat.

2. Sauté onions until golden brown.

3. Add garlic and ginger, and cook for 1-2 minutes.

4. Add chopped tomatoes and cook until soft.

5. Stir in turmeric, cumin, and coriander powders.

6. Add cubed potatoes and mix well.

7. Pour in coconut milk and water, and bring to a boil.

8. Reduce heat and simmer until the potatoes are tender.

9. Add cooked chickpeas and mix well.

10. Season with salt and pepper.

11. Serve hot with rice or chapati.

SALADS

Tanzanian salads are notable for their vibrant ingredients and refreshing flavors, setting them apart from other side dishes in the cuisine. These salads often combine raw vegetables like tomatoes, cucumbers, and onions with citrus dressings or coconut milk, creating a burst of flavor that complements the main dishes. The inclusion of fresh, locally-sourced produce not only enhances the taste but also boosts the nutritional value, providing essential vitamins and minerals.

The versatility of Tanzanian salads is evident in their ability to adapt to a range of culinary contexts, from casual meals to festive gatherings. They can be simple, focusing on a few key ingredients, or complex, incorporating grains like rice or legumes for a more filling option. This adaptability makes them a perfect accompaniment to both meat-based and vegetarian meals, enhancing the overall dining experience.

Salads in Tanzanian cuisine are celebrated not only for their delightful flavors but also for their role in promoting a healthy lifestyle. They provide a light, nutritious option that balances the richer, more indulgent components of a meal.

KACHUMBARI (TOMATO AND ONION SALAD)

Ingredients

- Tomato - 4, chopped.
- Onion - 1, finely sliced.
- Cucumber - 1, diced.
- Green chili - 1, chopped (optional).

- Lemon juice - 2 tbsp.
- Salt - to taste.
- Cilantro - 1/4 cup, chopped.

Instructions

1. In a large bowl, combine chopped tomatoes, finely sliced onion, and diced cucumber.

2. Add chopped green chili, if using.

3. Drizzle with lemon juice and season with salt.

4. Mix well and garnish with chopped cilantro.

5. Serve chilled.

CUCUMBER SALAD

Ingredients

- Cucumber - 2, thinly sliced.
- Red onion - 1, thinly sliced.
- Yogurt - 1 cup.
- Lemon juice - 1 tbsp.
- Dill - 1 tbsp, chopped.
- Salt - to taste.
- Pepper - to taste.

Instructions

1. In a large bowl, combine thinly sliced cucumber and red onion.

2. In a small bowl, whisk together yogurt, lemon juice, chopped dill, salt, and pepper.

3. Pour the dressing over the cucumber and onion mixture.

4. Toss to coat well.

5. Serve chilled.

CARROT AND PINEAPPLE SALAD

Ingredients

- Carrot - 3, grated.
- Pineapple - 1 cup, diced.
- Raisins - 1/4 cup.
- Mayonnaise - 1/4 cup.
- Lemon juice - 1 tbsp.
- Salt - to taste.
- Pepper - to taste.

Instructions

1. In a large bowl, combine grated carrot, diced pineapple, and raisins.

2. In a small bowl, whisk together mayonnaise, lemon juice, salt, and pepper.

3. Pour the dressing over the carrot mixture.

4. Toss to coat well.

5. Serve chilled.

AVOCADO SALAD

Ingredients

- Avocado - 2, diced.
- Tomato - 2, chopped.
- Red onion - 1, finely chopped.
- Cucumber - 1, diced.
- Lemon juice - 2 tbsp.
- Olive oil - 1 tbsp.
- Salt - to taste.
- Pepper - to taste.
- Cilantro - 1/4 cup, chopped.

Instructions

1. In a large bowl, combine diced avocado, chopped tomatoes, finely chopped red onion, and diced cucumber.

2. Drizzle with lemon juice and olive oil.

3. Season with salt and pepper.

4. Mix well and garnish with chopped cilantro.

5. Serve immediately.

BEETROOT SALAD

Ingredients

- Beetroot - 3, cooked and diced.
- Red onion - 1, finely chopped.
- Apple - 1, diced.
- Olive oil - 2 tbsp.
- Lemon juice - 1 tbsp.
- Salt - to taste.

- Pepper - to taste.
- Parsley - 1/4 cup, chopped.

Instructions

1. In a large bowl, combine cooked and diced beetroot, finely chopped red onion, and diced apple.

2. Drizzle with olive oil and lemon juice.

3. Season with salt and pepper.

4. Mix well and garnish with chopped parsley.

5. Serve chilled.

CABBAGE SALAD

Ingredients

- Cabbage - 1/2 head, shredded.
- Carrot - 1, grated.
- Red onion - 1, thinly sliced.
- Mayonnaise - 1/4 cup.
- Lemon juice - 1 tbsp.
- Salt - to taste.
- Pepper - to taste.

Instructions

1. In a large bowl, combine shredded cabbage, grated carrot, and thinly sliced red onion.

2. In a small bowl, whisk together mayonnaise, lemon juice, salt, and pepper.

3. Pour the dressing over the cabbage mixture.

4. Toss to coat well.

5. Serve chilled.

BANANA SALAD

Ingredients

- Bananas - 3, sliced.
- Lemon juice - 2 tbsp.
- Peanut butter - 1/4 cup.
- Honey - 2 tbsp.
- Yogurt - 1/2 cup.
- Salt - a pinch.

Instructions

1. In a large bowl, combine sliced bananas and lemon juice.

2. In a small bowl, mix together peanut butter, honey, yogurt, and a pinch of salt.

3. Pour the dressing over the bananas.

4. Toss gently to coat.

5. Serve immediately.

EGGPLANT SALAD

Ingredients

- Eggplant - 1, roasted and diced.
- Tomato - 2, chopped.
- Red onion - 1, finely chopped.
- Garlic - 2 cloves, minced.

- Lemon juice - 2 tbsp.
- Olive oil - 2 tbsp.
- Salt - to taste.
- Pepper - to taste.
- Parsley - 1/4 cup, chopped.

Instructions

1. In a large bowl, combine roasted and diced eggplant, chopped tomatoes, and finely chopped red onion.

2. Add minced garlic.

3. Drizzle with lemon juice and olive oil.

4. Season with salt and pepper.

5. Mix well and garnish with chopped parsley.

6. Serve chilled.

GREEN BEAN SALAD

Ingredients

- Green beans - 2 cups, blanched and chopped.
- Red bell pepper - 1, chopped.
- Red onion - 1, finely chopped.
- Garlic - 2 cloves, minced.
- Lemon juice - 2 tbsp.
- Olive oil - 2 tbsp.
- Salt - to taste.
- Pepper - to taste.

Instructions

1. In a large bowl, combine blanched and chopped green

beans, chopped red bell pepper, and finely chopped red onion.

2. Add minced garlic.

3. Drizzle with lemon juice and olive oil.

4. Season with salt and pepper.

5. Toss to coat well.

6. Serve chilled.

POTATO SALAD

Ingredients

- Potatoes - 4, boiled and diced.
- Egg - 2, hard-boiled and chopped.
- Red onion - 1, finely chopped.
- Pickles - 1/4 cup, chopped.
- Mayonnaise - 1/2 cup.
- Mustard - 1 tbsp.
- Salt - to taste.
- Pepper - to taste.
- Parsley - 1/4 cup, chopped.

Instructions

1. In a large bowl, combine boiled and diced potatoes, chopped hard-boiled eggs, finely chopped red onion, and chopped pickles.

2. In a small bowl, whisk together mayonnaise, mustard, salt, and pepper.

3. Pour the dressing over the potato mixture.

4. Toss to coat well.

5. Garnish with chopped parsley.

6. Serve chilled.

DESSERTS

Tanzanian desserts are distinguished by their use of natural sweeteners and fresh, local ingredients, setting them apart from the more heavily processed sweets found in other cuisines. These treats often incorporate fruits like mangoes, coconuts, and bananas, which not only offer a rich source of natural sugars but also essential vitamins and minerals. The inclusion of spices such as cinnamon and cardamom adds a unique depth of flavor while enhancing the health benefits of these desserts.

The versatility of Tanzanian desserts is showcased in the variety of forms they take, from simple fresh fruit salads to more elaborate dishes like mandazi, a type of fried bread. These desserts can be adapted to fit a range of occasions, whether it's a casual family meal or a festive celebration. By focusing on wholesome ingredients, these sweets provide a satisfying end to any meal without the guilt typically associated with dessert.

Tanzanian desserts emphasize the natural sweetness and flavors of their components, promoting a healthier approach to sweets. They are a delightful conclusion to dining, highlighting the culinary creativity and rich ingredient palette of Tanzania.

MANDAZI

Ingredients

- Flour - 2 cups.
- Sugar - 1/2 cup.
- Coconut milk - 1 cup.
- Baking powder - 1 tsp.
- Cardamom powder - 1/2 tsp.

- Salt - a pinch.
- Oil - for frying.

Instructions

1. In a large bowl, mix flour, sugar, baking powder, cardamom powder, and salt.

2. Gradually add coconut milk and mix to form a soft dough.

3. Roll out the dough on a floured surface to about 1/4 inch thickness.

4. Cut into desired shapes.

5. Heat oil in a deep frying pan over medium heat.

6. Fry the dough pieces until golden brown on both sides.

7. Drain on paper towels.

8. Serve warm.

KASHATA

Ingredients

- Sugar - 1 cup.
- Water - 1/4 cup.
- Grated coconut - 1 cup.
- Peanuts - 1/2 cup, roasted and chopped.
- Cardamom powder - 1/2 tsp.

Instructions

1. In a saucepan, combine sugar and water.

2. Cook over medium heat until the sugar dissolves and the syrup thickens.

3. Add grated coconut, roasted peanuts, and cardamom powder.

4. Stir well and cook until the mixture is thick and sticky.

5. Pour the mixture onto a greased surface and spread evenly.

6. Allow to cool and harden.

7. Cut into squares or desired shapes.

8. Serve and enjoy.

VITUMBUA

Ingredients

- Rice flour - 1 cup.
- Coconut milk - 1 cup.
- Sugar - 1/4 cup.
- Yeast - 1 tsp.
- Cardamom powder - 1/2 tsp.
- Salt - a pinch.
- Oil - for frying.

Instructions

1. In a bowl, mix rice flour, coconut milk, sugar, yeast, cardamom powder, and salt to form a batter.

2. Cover the bowl and let the batter rise for about an hour.

3. Heat oil in an appam pan or similar pan over medium heat.

4. Pour spoonfuls of the batter into the pan wells.

5. Cook until golden brown on both sides.

6. Remove and drain on paper towels.

7. Serve warm.

COCONUT CAKE

Ingredients

- Flour - 1 1/2 cups.
- Sugar - 1 cup.
- Butter - 1/2 cup, softened.
- Eggs - 2.
- Coconut milk - 1 cup.
- Baking powder - 1 tsp.
- Grated coconut - 1 cup.
- Vanilla extract - 1 tsp.
- Salt - a pinch.

Instructions

1. Preheat the oven to 350°F (175°C).

2. Grease and flour a baking pan.

3. In a bowl, cream together butter and sugar until light and fluffy.

4. Beat in eggs one at a time.

5. Stir in vanilla extract.

6. In another bowl, sift together flour, baking powder, and salt.

7. Gradually add the dry ingredients to the wet mixture, alternating with coconut milk.

8. Fold in grated coconut.

9. Pour the batter into the prepared pan.

10. Bake for 30-35 minutes or until a toothpick inserted into the center comes out clean.

11. Allow to cool before serving.

BANANA CAKE

Ingredients

- Flour - 1 1/2 cups.
- Sugar - 1 cup.
- Butter - 1/2 cup, softened.
- Eggs - 2.
- Bananas - 3, mashed.
- Baking powder - 1 tsp.
- Cinnamon powder - 1/2 tsp.
- Vanilla extract - 1 tsp.
- Salt - a pinch.

Instructions

1. Preheat the oven to 350°F (175°C).

2. Grease and flour a baking pan.

3. In a bowl, cream together butter and sugar until light and fluffy.

4. Beat in eggs one at a time.

5. Stir in vanilla extract.

6. In another bowl, sift together flour, baking powder, cinnamon, and salt.

7. Gradually add the dry ingredients to the wet mixture.

8. Fold in mashed bananas.

9. Pour the batter into the prepared pan.

10. Bake for 30-35 minutes or until a toothpick inserted into the center comes out clean.

11. Allow to cool before serving.

SWEET POTATO BALLS

Ingredients

- Sweet potatoes - 2 cups, boiled and mashed.
- Sugar - 1/4 cup.
- Coconut - 1/2 cup, grated.
- Cardamom powder - 1/2 tsp.
- Flour - 1/4 cup.
- Oil - for frying.

Instructions

1. In a large bowl, mix boiled and mashed sweet potatoes, sugar, grated coconut, and cardamom powder.

2. Add flour and mix to form a dough.

3. Shape the dough into small balls.

4. Heat oil in a deep frying pan over medium heat.

5. Fry the sweet potato balls until golden brown on all sides.

6. Drain on paper towels.

7. Serve warm.

MAANDAZI

Ingredients

- Flour - 2 cups.
- Sugar - 1/2 cup.
- Coconut milk - 1 cup.
- Baking powder - 1 tsp.
- Cardamom powder - 1/2 tsp.
- Salt - a pinch.
- Oil - for frying.

Instructions

1. In a large bowl, mix flour, sugar, baking powder, cardamom powder, and salt.

2. Gradually add coconut milk and mix to form a soft dough.

3. Roll out the dough on a floured surface to about 1/4 inch thickness.

4. Cut into desired shapes.

5. Heat oil in a deep frying pan over medium heat.

6. Fry the dough pieces until golden brown on both sides.

7. Drain on paper towels.

8. Serve warm.

FRIED BANANAS

Ingredients

- Bananas - 4, ripe but firm.
- Flour - 1/2 cup.
- Sugar - 2 tbsp.
- Milk - 1/4 cup.
- Egg - 1, beaten.
- Cinnamon powder - 1/2 tsp.
- Oil - for frying.

Instructions

1. Peel the bananas and cut them in half lengthwise.

2. In a bowl, mix flour, sugar, and cinnamon powder.

3. In another bowl, whisk together milk and beaten egg.

4. Dip each banana piece in the milk mixture, then coat with the flour mixture.

5. Heat oil in a frying pan over medium heat.

6. Fry the bananas until golden brown on all sides.

7. Drain on paper towels.

8. Serve warm.

HALWA (SWEETMEAT)

Ingredients

- Sugar - 1 cup.
- Water - 1/2 cup.
- Cornstarch - 1/4 cup.
- Ghee - 1/4 cup.
- Cardamom powder - 1/2 tsp.
- Nuts - 1/4 cup, chopped (optional).
- Food coloring - a few drops (optional).

Instructions

1. In a saucepan, combine sugar and water.

2. Cook over medium heat until the sugar dissolves and the syrup thickens.

3. In a bowl, mix cornstarch with a little water to make a smooth paste.

4. Add the cornstarch paste to the sugar syrup and stir continuously.

5. Add ghee and continue to stir until the mixture thickens and starts to leave the sides of the pan.

6. Stir in cardamom powder, chopped nuts, and food coloring, if using.

7. Pour the mixture into a greased dish and spread evenly.

8. Allow to cool and set.

9. Cut into squares or desired shapes.

10. Serve and enjoy.

UJI (PORRIDGE)

Ingredients

- Millet flour - 1 cup.
- Water - 4 cups.
- Sugar - 1/4 cup (optional).
- Milk - 1 cup (optional).
- Salt - a pinch.

Instructions

1. In a bowl, mix millet flour with a little water to make a smooth paste.

2. In a pot, bring the remaining water to a boil.

3. Gradually add the millet paste to the boiling water, stirring continuously to avoid lumps.

4. Reduce heat and simmer until the porridge thickens, stirring occasionally.

5. Add sugar and salt, and continue to cook for a few more minutes.

6. Stir in milk if desired, and cook until heated through.

7. Serve hot.

CHAPATI WITH HONEY

Ingredients

- Flour - 2 cups.

- Water - 1 cup.
- Salt - 1/2 tsp.
- Oil - 2 tbsp.
- Honey - for serving.

Instructions

1. In a large bowl, mix flour and salt.

2. Gradually add water and mix to form a soft dough.

3. Knead the dough for about 10 minutes until smooth and elastic.

4. Divide the dough into small balls and roll out each ball into a thin circle.

5. Heat a skillet over medium heat and cook each chapati for 1-2 minutes on each side until golden brown.

6. Brush with oil while cooking.

7. Serve warm with honey drizzled on top.

RICE PUDDING

Ingredients

- Rice - 1/2 cup.
- Coconut milk - 2 cups.
- Sugar - 1/2 cup.
- Cardamom powder - 1/2 tsp.
- Raisins - 1/4 cup.
- Water - 1 cup.

Instructions

1. In a pot, combine rice and water. Bring to a boil.

2. Reduce heat and simmer until the rice is cooked and the water is absorbed.

3. Add coconut milk, sugar, and cardamom powder to the pot.

4. Stir well and cook over low heat until the mixture thickens.

5. Add raisins and cook for a few more minutes.

6. Serve warm or chilled.

TAMARIND CANDY

Ingredients

- Tamarind pulp - 1 cup.
- Sugar - 1 cup.
- Water - 1/2 cup.
- Cardamom powder - 1/2 tsp.
- Salt - a pinch.

Instructions

1. In a saucepan, combine tamarind pulp, sugar, and water.

2. Cook over medium heat until the mixture thickens and starts to leave the sides of the pan.

3. Add cardamom powder and salt, and mix well.

4. Pour the mixture onto a greased surface and spread evenly.

5. Allow to cool and harden.

6. Cut into squares or desired shapes.

7. Serve and enjoy.

SWEET BREAD

Ingredients

- Flour - 2 cups.
- Sugar - 1/2 cup.
- Yeast - 1 tsp.
- Milk - 1 cup, warm.
- Butter - 2 tbsp, melted.
- Egg - 1.
- Salt - 1/2 tsp.

Instructions

1. In a large bowl, combine flour, sugar, yeast, and salt.

2. Add warm milk, melted butter, and egg. Mix to form a soft dough.

3. Knead the dough for about 10 minutes until smooth and elastic.

4. Cover the dough and let it rise in a warm place for about 1 hour.

5. Preheat the oven to 350°F (175°C).

6. Shape the dough into a loaf and place it in a greased

loaf pan.

7. Bake for 30-35 minutes until golden brown.

8. Allow to cool before slicing and serving.

PEANUT BRITTLE

Ingredients

- Sugar - 1 cup.
- Peanuts - 1 cup, roasted and chopped.
- Butter - 2 tbsp.
- Salt - a pinch.
- Baking soda - 1/2 tsp.

Instructions

1. In a saucepan, melt butter over medium heat.

2. Add sugar and stir continuously until it melts and turns golden brown.

3. Quickly stir in chopped peanuts, salt, and baking soda.

4. Pour the mixture onto a greased surface and spread evenly.

5. Allow to cool and harden.

6. Break into pieces and serve.

RECIPE LIST

BREAKFASTS

CHAPATI 9
MANDAZI 10
VITUMBUA (RICE PANCAKES) 11
UJI (PORRIDGE) 11
MAANDAZI 12
NDIZI KAANGA (FRIED BANANAS) 13
MAHAMRI (COCONUT DOUGHNUTS) 13
MBAAZI (PIGEON PEAS IN COCONUT SAUCE) 14
KASHATA (COCONUT AND PEANUT BARS) 15
BAGIA ZA DENGU (LENTIL FRITTERS) 16

APPETIZERS

MISHKAKI (SKEWERS) 17
SAMAKI WA KUPAKA (COCONUT FISH) 18
BAJIA (CHICKPEA FRITTERS) 19
KACHORI (SPICED POTATO BALLS) 20
MEAT SAMBUSA 21
MCHICHA (SPINACH AND PEANUT CURRY) 22
NDIZI NYAMA (PLANTAINS WITH MEAT) 23
ACHARI (PICKLED MANGO) 24
BHAJIA ZA DENGU (LENTIL FRITTERS) 25
PWEZA WA NAZI (OCTOPUS IN COCONUT) 26

SOUPS

- MTORI (BANANA AND BEEF SOUP) 27
- SUPU YA NDIZI (PLANTAIN SOUP) 28
- SUPU YA KUKU (CHICKEN SOUP) 29
- DENGU SOUP (LENTIL SOUP) 30
- NYAMA YA KUSAGA SOUP (GROUND MEAT SOUP) 31
- UROJO (ZANZIBAR SOUP) 32
- MAKANGE YA NYAMA (SPICED BEEF SOUP) 33
- SAMAKI SOUP (FISH SOUP) 34
- SUPU YA VIAZI (POTATO SOUP) 36
- SUPU YA KARANGA (PEANUT SOUP) 37
- MBAAZI SOUP (PIGEON PEA SOUP) 38
- NG'OMBE SOUP (BEEF BONE SOUP) 39
- KAMBA NA NAZI (PRAWN AND COCONUT SOUP) 40
- MCHUZI WA BIRINGANI (EGGPLANT STEW) 41
- SUPU YA MATUMBO (TRIPE SOUP) 42

STEWS

- NYAMA CHOMA (GRILLED MEAT) 43
- MCHUZI WA SAMAKI (FISH CURRY) 44
- MCHUZI WA NYAMA (BEEF CURRY) 45
- OCTOPUS CURRY 46
- MCHUZI WA KUKU (CHICKEN CURRY) 48
- BOKO BOKO HAREES (WHEAT, MEAT PORRIDGE) 49
- MCHUZI WA MBUZI (GOAT CURRY) 50
- MCHUZI WA DENGU (LENTIL STEW) 51

KUKU PAKA (CHICKEN IN COCONUT) 52
MCHUZI WA BIRINGANI (EGGPLANT STEW) 53
MCHUZI WA NAZI (COCONUT SAUCE) 54
MCHUZI WA PWEZA (OCTOPUS CURRY) 55
BAMIA (OKRA STEW) 56
KAMBA MCHUZI (PRAWN CURRY) 57
MCHUZI WA KAMBA (SHRIMP STEW) 58

BEEF DISHES
NYAMA CHOMA 60
PILAU (SPICED RICE WITH MEAT) 61
BIRYANI 62
BEEF KEBABS 64
BEEF SAMAKI 65
KITIMOTO (PORK) 66
NYAMA YA KUKAANGA (FRIED BEEF) 67
BEEF STEW 68
MKATE WA NYAMA (MEAT BREAD) 69
BEEF SUKUMA WIKI (BEEF WITH KALE) 70
BEEF AND POTATO CURRY 71
BEEF AND BANANA STEW 72
MSHIKAKI (MARINATED BEEF SKEWERS) 73
UGALI NA NYAMA (CORNMEAL WITH MEAT) 74
BEEF AND EGGPLANT STEW 75

PORK DISHES

KITIMOTO (FRIED PORK) 77
PORK RIBS 78
PORK STEW 79
CHOMA PORK (GRILLED PORK) 80
PORK CURRY 81
PORK CHOPS 82
PORK AND BEAN CASSEROLE 83
PORK PILAU 84
SWEET AND SOUR PORK 86
SPICY PORK STIR FRY 87
PORK AND PINEAPPLE CURRY 88
PORK AND VEGETABLE KEBABS 89
UGALI WITH PORK 90
PORK MCHUZI 91
SMOKED PORK 92

CHICKEN DISHES

KUKU PAKA 94
KUKU CHOMA (GRILLED CHICKEN) 96
CHICKEN PILAU 97
CHICKEN BIRYANI 98
KUKU NA NAZI (CHICKEN IN COCONUT SAUCE) 99
CHICKEN STEW 100
CHICKEN AND VEGETABLE STIR FRY 101
CHICKEN AND PEANUT STEW 102

FRIED CHICKEN 103
CHICKEN SUKUMA WIKI 104
CHICKEN AND POTATO CURRY 105
SPICED CHICKEN WINGS 106
CHICKEN AND RICE CASSEROLE 107
CHICKEN KEBABS 108
CHICKEN AND PLANTAIN CURRY 109

GOAT DISHES
MBUZI CHOMA (ROASTED GOAT) 111
GOAT CURRY 112
GOAT PILAU 113
GOAT BIRYANI 115
GOAT STEW 116
FRIED GOAT 117
GOAT AND VEGETABLE STIR FRY 118
GOAT AND PEANUT STEW 119
GOAT KEBABS 120
GOAT AND BANANA CURRY 121
SPICED GOAT 122
GOAT AND RICE CASSEROLE 123
GOAT SUKUMA WIKI 124
GOAT AND POTATO STEW 125
SMOKED GOAT 126

SEAFOOD DISHES

SAMAKI WA KUPAKA (GRILLED FISH, COCONUT)...... 128
MCHUZI WA SAMAKI (FISH CURRY) 129
GRILLED PRAWNS 130
FISH BIRYANI... 131
FISH PILAU 132
OCTOPUS CURRY.. 134
FRIED FISH.. 135
FISH STEW 136
PRAWN CURRY.. 137
FISH AND VEGETABLE STIR FRY 138
SQUID CURRY.. 139
FISH AND COCONUT SOUP....................................... 140
SEAFOOD MIXED GRILL 141
FISH KEBABS... 142
FISH AND BANANA CURRY 143

RICE DISHES

PILAU 145
WALI WA NAZI (COCONUT RICE).............................. 147
BIRYANI 147
WALI WA KUKAANGA (FRIED RICE) 149
WALI NA SAMAKI (RICE WITH FISH)........................ 150
WALI NA MAHARAGE (RICE WITH BEANS) 151
WALI WA KAROTI (CARROT RICE) 152
WALI WA ZAFARANI (SAFFRON RICE) 153

WALI WA TENDE (DATE RICE) 154
WALI WA KUNDE (COWPEA RICE) 155

BEANS

MAHARAGE YA NAZI (BEANS IN COCONUT SAUCE) .. 157
MAHARAGE (RED KIDNEY BEANS STEW) 158
FRIED BEANS 159
BEAN SOUP 160
BEAN STEW 161
BEANS AND VEGETABLES 162
BEAN CURRY 163
BEANS WITH SPINACH 164
BEANS AND RICE 165
BEANS AND BANANA STEW 166
SWEET BEANS 167
SPICY BEANS 168
BEANS AND CORN 169
BEANS AND POTATO STEW 170
BEANS AND TOMATO SAUCE 171

LEGUMES

DENGU (LENTIL CURRY) 173
CHICKPEA CURRY 174
PIGEON PEA STEW 176
LENTIL SOUP 177
CHICKPEA SALAD 178

LENTIL AND VEGETABLE STIR FRY	179
PIGEON PEAS AND RICE	180
LENTIL PILAU	181
CHICKPEA STEW	182
PIGEON PEA SOUP	183
LENTIL AND BANANA STEW	184
CHICKPEA AND SPINACH STEW	185
LENTILS WITH COCONUT	186
PIGEON PEAS AND BANANA CURRY	187
CHICKPEA AND POTATO CURRY	189

SALADS

KACHUMBARI (TOMATO AND ONION SALAD)	191
CUCUMBER SALAD	192
CARROT AND PINEAPPLE SALAD	193
AVOCADO SALAD	194
BEETROOT SALAD	194
CABBAGE SALAD	195
BANANA SALAD	196
EGGPLANT SALAD	196
GREEN BEAN SALAD	197
POTATO SALAD	198

DESSERTS

MANDAZI	200
KASHATA	201

VITUMBUA	202
COCONUT CAKE	203
BANANA CAKE	204
SWEET POTATO BALLS	205
MAANDAZI	206
FRIED BANANAS	207
HALWA (SWEETMEAT)	208
UJI (PORRIDGE)	209
CHAPATI WITH HONEY	209
RICE PUDDING	210
TAMARIND CANDY	211
SWEET BREAD	212
PEANUT BRITTLE	213

Printed in Great Britain
by Amazon